VISUAL STUDIO 2019
VB.NET AND
REPORTS.RDLC

Working with the OLEDB and the Dataset

Richard Thomas Edwards

Introduction

Hello. Welcome to learning how to create reports in VB.Net. Have I got a real treat for you! This book is dedicated to using Visual Studio 2019 Community Edition. Now, I've seen where a lot of programmers are having issues creating reports. While it was an issue for even mighty Microsoft to resolve. This book not only fixes the issue, it takes reporting through VB.Net to a new level.

Imagine for a moment, you don't need a to have anything but reports – yes, that's plural – and the code, using OleDb to make the reports work.

In fact, imagine being able dynamically create all the code needed to create reports – including the code that becomes the reports – using VB.Net and OLEDB.

Well this book makes all that imagination a reality.

This book is broken down into two sections. The first section is designed to work through the various ways you can create the reports. The second describes the various parts that create the reports from xml to each segment of the report that can be automated and save you time.

Now, I know a lot of people claim they can save you time. But never tell you how much time. I can tell you that it took less than a minute to create three reports – 2009 lines each and the code needed to populate the reports – 267 lines of code.

I just added all of the code to a new Visual Studio 2019 VB.Net, put a tab control onto the form, added a ReportViewer for each tab and run the program in less than ten minutes.

Here's what it looks like:

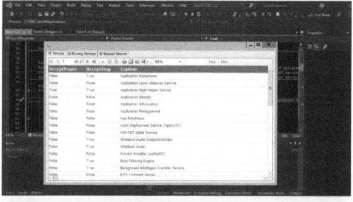

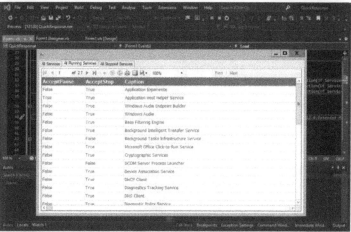

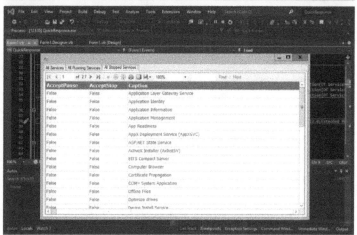

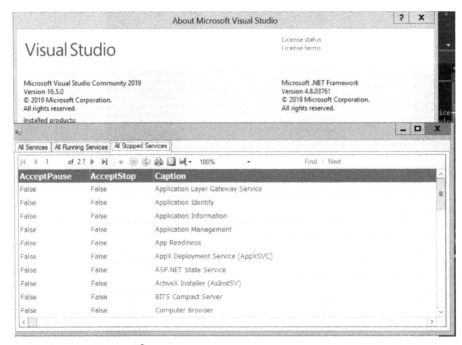

Is that tough enough?

Let's go to work.

Creating your first project
If you have used Visual Studio in the past get
ready for a shocker!

I can't tell you how to install Visual Studio 2019 for two reasons. First, it would take up a large amount of space in this book to do so and, second, it has a pretty straight forward installation wizard. Just remember, if this is your first time installing Visual Studio 2019 Community edition that you need to include:

Desktop & Mobile (5)

.NET desktop development
Build WPF, Windows Forms, and console applications using
C#, Visual Basic, and F# with .NET Core and .NET...

Otherwise, you won't have anything to work with when you need to create a Windows Form application.

Also, once it is installed, you're going to want to install the ReportViewer for Visual Studio 2019. To do this, just follow this link.

If you have used Visual Studio in the past, you've probably gotten used to seeing something like this as soon as you start Visual Studio you generally see this:

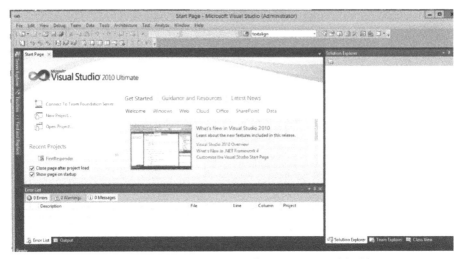

Or something close to it. Well, Visual Studio 2019 starts with this:

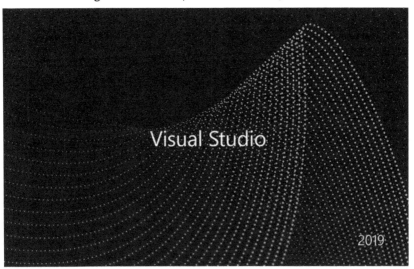

And then, goes directly into this:

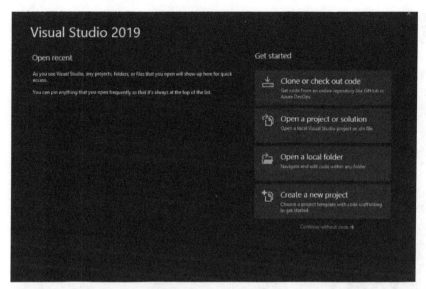

Since we're going to be creating a new project, the last option: Create a new project; is the one we want to use. There is more confusion to follow:

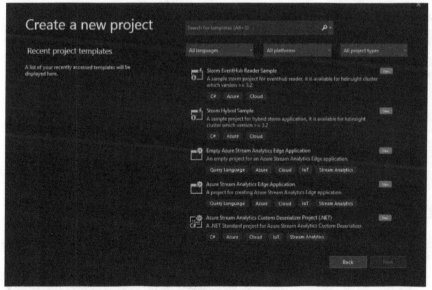

Where it says All languages, select VB.Net. Where it says All platforms, select Windows. Where it says All project types, select Desktop. You should now see this:

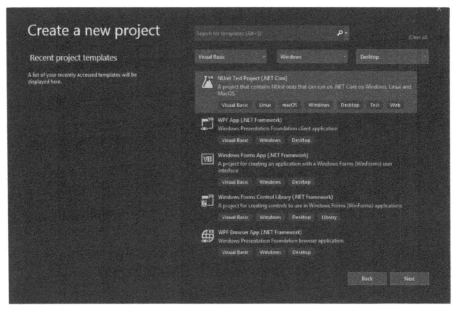

Okay, so now we want to select Windows Form App(.Net Framework). If you double click on that option, you don't have to click next.

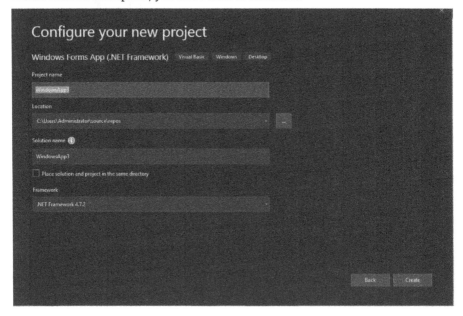

Name your project, select a different location, change the solution name and decide what framework you want to use. Those are your options. Please take note.

If you have been programming for years, you know that our favorite location for our work has always been in the documents area. Not anymore. On my machine it is C:\Users\Administrator\source\repos.

Once your application has been created and the blank form is ready to go, go to the left side of the IDE where it says toolbox and click on the Toolbox. Once expanded, right click and choose Chose Items:

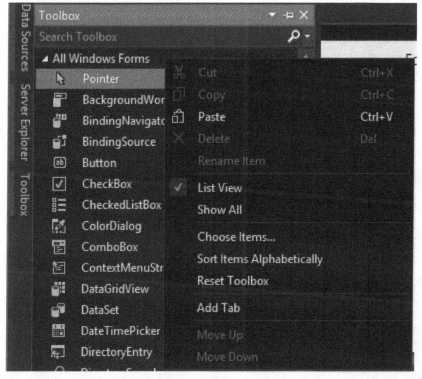

Once you've selected that, another window will popup. Wait a minute and click on the Namespace column header listbox. Then look for OleDbComponents and select the OleDBCommand, OleDbConnection and OleDbDataAdapter and then click okay.

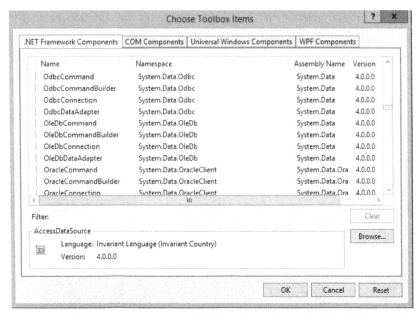

Once these components are added to the toolbox, double click on each to add them to your form. It should look like this:

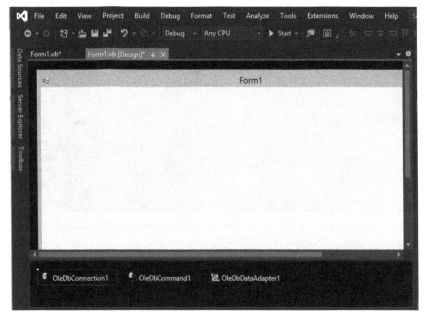

Normally, I just write the code out to make all of this work...but, is there any documentation on this?

Anyway, the next step is to create a connection string. Let's start there.

So, I right click on the OleDbConnection object and select properties:

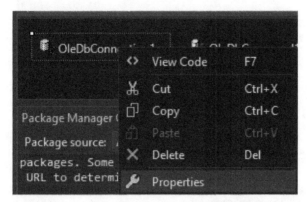

Normally, I would simply select a provider, search for a Data Source an that composite would become my connection string. Well....the guys or girls who decided that they would delete all programmer's methods to create a connection string decided, instead that the connection string option was the only way to create one.

So, I went to the far right of the connection string and clicked on the dropdown icon and selected <New Connection>..:

Add Connection ? X

Enter information to connect to the selected data source or click "Change" to choose a different data source and/or provider.

Data source:

| Microsoft Access Database File (OLE DB) | Change... |

Database file name:

| | Browse... |

Log on to the database

User name: Admin

Password:

☐ Save my password

Advanced...

| Test Connection | OK | Cancel |

Up to this point, I start questioning things. Like the fact that up until now, OleDb was pretty much for OleDb and there was a distinct separation between OleDb and Odbc. Primarily because Odbc has its own set of drivers. Furthermore, by default the OleDb provider for Odbc has been the default provider for ADO since its conception.

So, I thought, what the heck, I'll use it just to see what happens.

I browsed for my 25 year old NWind database, tested the connection and it worked.

I then right clicked on the command and went to properties:

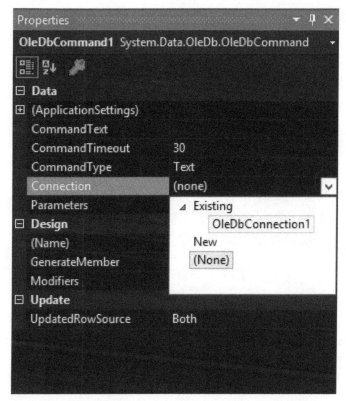

I then bound the Command to the Connection and then went to the far right corner of the CommandText and it came up with this:

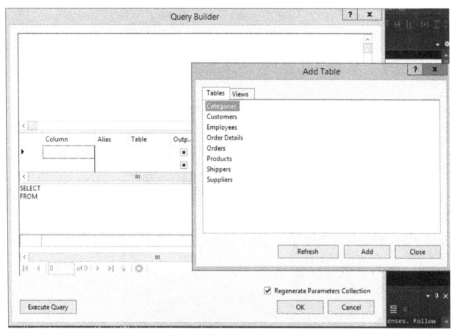

So, I went with products, selected all columns and clicked ok.

I also made sure the connection, command and dataadapter were bound to each other and then wrote the following code in the form load:

```
Imports System.Data
Public Class Form1
    Private Sub Form1_Load(sender As Object, e As EventArgs) Handles MyBase.Load

        Dim ds As New System.Data.DataSet
        OleDbDataAdapter1.Fill(ds)
        DataGridView1.DataSource = ds.Tables(0)

    End Sub
End Class
```

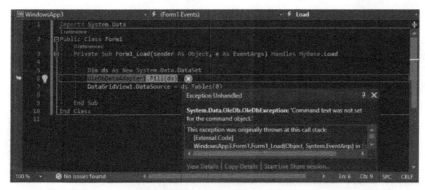

In the time that it took me to realize all of this was broken, I could have been done writing the code below and showing you how easy it is to create the reports.

```
Imports System.Data.OleDb
Public Class Form1
    Private Sub Form1_Load(sender As Object, e As EventArgs) Handles MyBase.Load

        Dim cn As New OleDbConnection
        cn.ConnectionString = "Provider=Microsoft.Jet.OleDb.4.0;Data Source=C:\NWIND.MDB"
        cn.Open()
        Dim cmd As New OleDb.OleDbCommand()
        cmd.Connection = cn
        cmd.CommandType = System.Data.CommandType.Text
        cmd.CommandText = "Select * from products"
        cmd.ExecuteNonQuery()

        Dim da As New OleDbDataAdapter(cmd)
        Dim ds As New System.Data.DataSet
        da.Fill(ds)
        DataGridView1.DataSource = ds.Tables(0)

    End Sub

End Class
```

Here's the visual output:

ProductID	ProductName	SupplierID	CategoryID	QuantityPerUnit	UnitPrice	UnitsInStock	UnitsOr ^
1	Chai	1	1	10 boxes x 20 bags	18	39	0
2	Chang	1	1	24 - 12 oz bottles	19	17	40
3	Aniseed Syrup	1	2	12 - 550 ml bottles	10	13	70
4	Chef Anton's Caj...	2	2	48 - 6 oz jars	22	53	0
5	Chef Anton's Gu...	2	2	36 boxes	21.35	0	0
6	Grandma's Boyse...	3	2	12 - 8 oz jars	25	120	0
7	Uncle Bob's Orga...	3	7	12 - 1 lb pkgs.	30	15	0
8	Northwoods Cran...	3	2	12 - 12 oz jars	40	6	0
9	Mishi Kobe Niku	4	6	18 - 500 g pkgs.	97	29	0
10	Ikura	4	8	12 - 200 ml jars	31	31	0
11	Queso Cabrales	5	4	1 kg pkg.	21	22	30
12	Queso Mancheg...	5	4	10 - 500 g pkgs	38	86	0
13	Konbu	6	8	2 kg box	6	24	0
14	Tofu	6	7	40 - 100 g pkgs.	23.25	35	0
15	Genen Shouyu	6	2	24 - 250 ml bottles	15.5	39	0
16	Pavlova	7	3	32 - 500 g boxes	17.45	29	0
17	Alice Mutton	7	6	20 - 1 kg tins	39	0	0
18	Carnarvon Tigers	7	8	16 kg pkg.	62.5	42	0
19	Teatime Chocolat...	8	3	10 boxes x 2 pie...	9.2	25	0

As for the Odbc code being used in OleDb:

```
Imports System.Data.OleDb
Public Class Form1
    Private Sub Form1_Load(sender As Object, e As EventArgs) Handles MyBase.Load

        Dim cn As New OleDbConnection
        cn.ConnectionString = "Provider=MSDASQL; Driver={Microsoft Access Driver (*.mdb); dbq=C:\nwind.mdb"
        cn.Open()
        Dim cmd As New OleDb.OleDbCommand()
        cmd.Connection = cn
        cmd.CommandType = System.Data.CommandType.Text
        cmd.CommandText = "Select * from products"
        cmd.ExecuteNonQuery()

        Dim da As New OleDbDataAdapter(cmd)
        Dim ds As New System.Data.DataSet
        da.Fill(ds)
        DataGridView1.DataSource = ds.Tables(0)

    End Sub
```

End Class

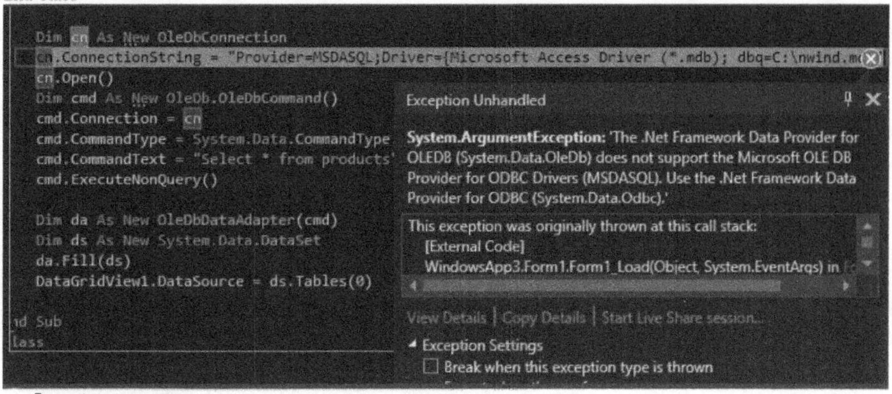
Dim cn As New OleDbConnection
cn.ConnectionString = "Provider=MSDASQL;Driver={Microsoft Access Driver (*.mdb); dbq=C:\nwind.m
cn.Open()
Dim cmd As New OleDb.OleDbCommand()
cmd.Connection = cn
cmd.CommandType = System.Data.CommandType
cmd.CommandText = "Select * from products"
cmd.ExecuteNonQuery()
Dim da As New OleDbDataAdapter(cmd)
Dim ds As New System.Data.DataSet
da.Fill(ds)
DataGridView1.DataSource = ds.Tables(0)
Sub
Exception Unhandled
System.ArgumentException: 'The .Net Framework Data Provider for OLEDB (System.Data.OleDb) does not support the Microsoft OLE DB Provider for ODBC Drivers (MSDASQL). Use the .Net Framework Data Provider for ODBC (System.Data.Odbc).'
This exception was originally thrown at this call stack:
[External Code]
WindowsApp3.Form1.Form1_Load(Object, System.EventArgs) in
View Details | Copy Details | Start Live Share session...
Exception Settings
Break when this exception type is thrown

I rest my case.

An alternative approach to working with older Access Databases

Just skip this if you don't want to make your life easier when you have to create a report from an older version of an Access Database

The reason why I am putting this in front of the normal OleDb coding examples is there is a lot of companies still using the older versions of Access and because it is about the simplest code you can possibly write and because I'm also using an older version of Access.

STEP #1: CREATE THE ELEMENT XML

Basically, what we want to do is convert the table into a simple element xml file. So, I created a module that is so generic all you have to do is pass over to it an ADODB.Recordset and the tablename.

```
Module ModConverter

    Public Sub Create_Element_XML(ByVal rs As Object, ByVal Tablename As String)

        Dim fso As Object = CreateObject("Scripting.FileSystemObject")
        Dim txtstream As Object = fso.OpenTextFile(Application.StartupPath & "\" & Tablename & ".xml", 2, True, -2)

        txtstream.WriteLine("<?xml version=""1.0"" encoding=""ISO-8859-1""?>")
        txtstream.WriteLine("<data>")
```

```
   rs.MoveLast()
   rs.Movefirst()

Do While Not rs.eof
   txtstream.WriteLine("<" & Tablename & ">")
   For x As Integer = 0 To rs.Fields.count - 1
      If IsDBNull(rs.Fields(x).Value) = False Then
         Try
            Dim Value As String = rs.Fields(x).Value
            Value = Trim(Value)
            Value = Replace(Value, Chr(34), "")
            txtstream.WriteLine("<" & rs.Fields(x).Name & ">" & Value & "</" & rs.Fields(x).Name & ">")
         Catch ex As Exception
            txtstream.WriteLine("<" & rs.Fields(x).Name & "/>")
         End Try
      End If
   Next
   txtstream.WriteLine("</" & Tablename & ">")
   rs.MoveNext()
Loop
txtstream.WriteLine("</data>")
txtstream.close()


   End Sub

End Module
```

In the form load, I created an ADODB.Recordset, sent the properties, decided to use the Products table and passed both of these variables over to the module's conversion routine.

```
Dim rs As Object = CreateObject("ADODB.Recordset")
rs.ActiveConnection = "Provider=Microsoft.Jet.OleDb.4.0;Data Source=C:\nwind.mdb"
rs.CursorLocation = 3
rs.Locktype = 3
rs.Source = "Select * from Products"
rs.Open()

ModConverter.Create_Element_XML(rs, "products")
```

After running that code, I commented it out created a new DataSet object, read in the newly created xml and used the writeSchemaXML routine to create the xsd file I will be using on the next step. The code to produce the xsd file is below:

```
Dim ds As New System.Data.DataSet
ds.ReadXml(Application.StartupPath & "\products.xml")
ds.WriteXmlSchema(Application.StartupPath & "\products.xsd")
```

STEP #2: IMPORT THE XML AND XSD FILES INTO THE PROJECT

At this point, I simply went to the IDE menu, selected project, then add existing Item, went over to the project, Bin and then debug where I found the two files after setting the extension to All Files(*.*) as shown below:

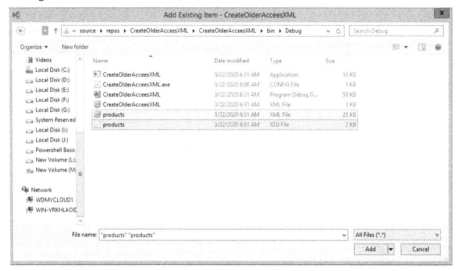

I highlighted both files and clicked Add. Now, both files are part of the project.

STEP #3: CREATE THE RDLC REPORT FILE

Next I needed to create the report. Heading back up to project, I then clicked on Add A New Item and decided to use the Report Wizard.

At this point, I go to the middle left option and click new.

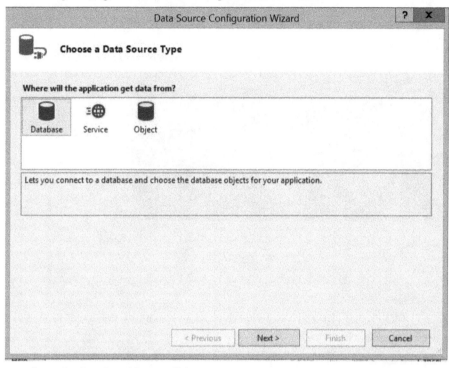

After selecting the Object, I click next.

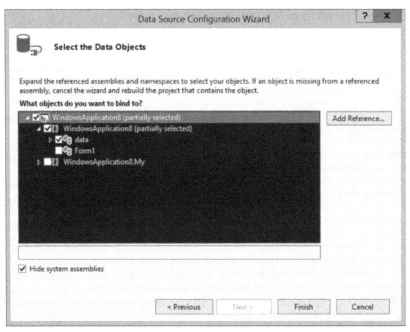

I want to use the xsd file here which is now part of the application. So, I selected it and clicked finish.

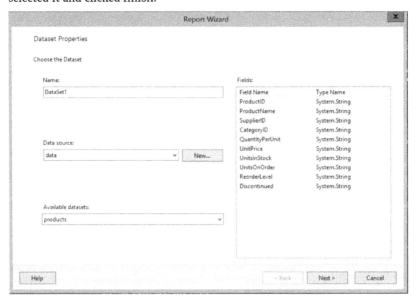

A couple of things to note. When I checked data in the previous window, neither data nor the fields showed up. Sometimes, get to this next step, the Data Source Combobox is populated with what I selected. But in this case, I had to click the ComboBox and select data as the Data Source option. The fields were then display as shown above. Also notice that products is defined as the dataset.

I click next and now I have to drag and drop all the field names into the values box as shown below.

After I'm done here, I click Next, Next and Finish.

My report is now ready to be Viewed.

Now, I'm willing to be you that you think I'm going to prove to you that this, too, is broken. Nope. Sorry to disappoint but I'm about to show you how I fixed it.

So, I go over to the toolbox search box and type in Report Viewer if it is found, I add it to the form. If it isn't I install a version of the report viewer and then add it to the form.

Either way, it isn't going to show up on the form.

Well, that doesn't stop me. If I haven't already mentioned this before now, I used to work for technical support at Microsoft. I was well know for tackling some of the hardest issues. So, I'm used to things being broken and fixing them.

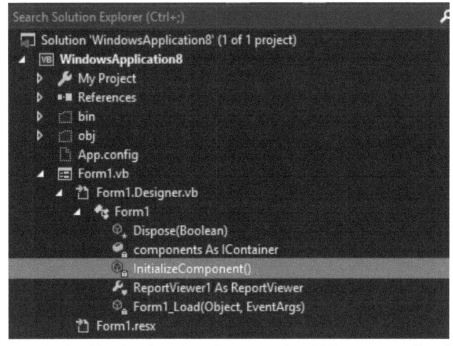

Notice that things here have changed. So, I open the InitializeComponent file and look for the issue. It is so blaringly obvious it almost jumps off the page. I see ReportViewer1 added correctly entry but where is the Me.Controls.Add(Me.ReportViewer1)?

```
Me.AutoScaleDimensions = New System.Drawing.SizeF(6.0!, 13.0!)
Me.AutoScaleMode = System.Windows.Forms.AutoScaleMode.Font
Me.ClientSize = New System.Drawing.Size(800, 450)
Me.Name = "Form1"
Me.Text = "Form1"
Me.ResumeLayout(False)
```

So, I added it.

```
'Form1
'
Me.AutoScaleDimensions = New System.Drawing.SizeF(6.0!, 13.0!)
Me.AutoScaleMode = System.Windows.Forms.AutoScaleMode.Font
Me.ClientSize = New System.Drawing.Size(800, 450)
Me.Name = "Form1"
Me.Text = "Form1"
Me.Controls.Add(Me.ReportViewer1)
Me.ResumeLayout(False)
```

And when I go back over to the form:

I set the docking property to fill and because the control thinks it is running, I write the code to reset it and have customized the view enough to make it look different.

```
Me.ReportViewer1.LocalReport.ReportPath =
"C:\Users\Administrator\Desktop\Basic\WindowsApplication8\WindowsApplication8\Report1.rdlc"
    Me.ReportViewer1.LocalReport.DataSources.Clear()
    Dim ds As New System.Data.DataSet

ds.ReadXml("C:\Users\Administrator\Desktop\Basic\WindowsApplication8\WindowsApplication8\products.xml")
    Me.ReportViewer1.LocalReport.DataSources.Add(New
Microsoft.Reporting.WinForms.ReportDataSource("DataSet1", ds.Tables(0)))
    Me.ReportViewer1.RefreshReport()
```

Here's the results:

Product ID	Product Name	Supplier ID	Category ID	Quantity Per Unit	Unit Price	Units In Stock	Units On Order	Reorder Level	Discontinued
1	Chai	1	1	10 boxes x 20 bags	18	39	0	10	False
2	Chang	1	1	24 - 12 oz bottles	19	17	40	25	False
3	Aniseed Syrup	1	2	12 - 550 ml bottles	10	13	70	25	False
4	Chef Anton's Cajun Seasoning	2	2	48 - 6 oz jars	22	53	0	0	False
5	Chef Anton's Gumbo Mix	2	2	36 boxes	21.35	0	0	0	True
6	Grandma's Boysenberry Spread	3	2	12 - 8 oz jars	25	120	0	25	False
7	Uncle Bob's Organic Dried Pears	3	7	12 - 1 lb pkgs.	30	15	0	10	False
8	Northwoods Cranberry Sauce	3	2	12 - 12 oz jars	40	6	0	0	False
9	Mishi Kobe Niku	4	6	18 - 500 g pkgs.	97	29	0	0	True
10	Ikura	4	8	12 - 200 ml jars	31	31	0	0	False
11	Queso Cabrales	5	4	1 kg pkg.	21	22	30	30	False
12	Queso Manchego La Pastora	5	4	10 - 500 g pkgs	38	86	0	0	False
13	Konbu	6	8	2 kg box	6	24	0	5	False
14	Tofu	6	7	40 - 100 g pkgs	23.25	35	0	0	False
15	Genen Shouyu	6	2	24 - 250 ml bottles	15.5	39	0	5	False
16	Pavlova	7	3	32 - 500 g boxes	17.45	29	0	10	False
17	Alice Mutton	7	6	20 - 1 kg tins	39	0	0	0	True
18	Carnarvon Tigers	7	8	16 kg pkg.	62.5	42	0	0	False
19	Teatime Chocolate Biscuits	8	3	10 boxes x 12 pieces	9.2	25	0	5	False
20	Sir Rodney's Marmalade	8	3	30 gift boxes	81	40	0	0	False
21	Sir Rodney's Scones	8	3	24 pkgs. x 4 pieces	10	3	40	5	False

I rest my case.

Let's move on.

The OLEDB Objects
Connection, Command, DataReader and DataAdapter

If there is only two things you remember from this book, it is the fact that all communications with a database and all records returned rely on a connection string and a query – could be a simple query, a query that uses joins or a stored procedure.

The examples in this book use both connection strings and simple queries. However, for the sake of creating templates, shown below, this book is using empty connection strings and queries.

```
Imports System.Data
Imports System.Data.OleDb

Module ModOLEDBConnectionOptions

    Public drr As OleDbDataReader
    Public da As OleDbDataAdapter

    Public Sub create_OleDb_Connection_Using_Connection_Command_And_DataAdapter(ByVal cnstr As String, ByVal strQuery As String)

        Dim cn As OleDbConnection = New OleDbConnection
        cn.ConnectionString = cnstr
        cn.Open()

        Dim cmd As OleDbCommand = New OleDbCommand()
        cmd.Connection = cn
        cmd.CommandType = System.Data.CommandType.Text
        cmd.ExecuteNonQuery()

        da = New OleDbDataAdapter(cmd)

    End Sub

    Public Sub create_OleDb_Connection_Using_Connection_And_DataAdapter(ByVal cnstr As String, ByVal strQuery As String)
```

```vb
    Dim cn As OleDbConnection = New OleDbConnection
    cn.ConnectionString = cnstr
    cn.Open()


    da = New OleDbDataAdapter(strQuery, cn)

End Sub

Public Sub create_OleDb_Connection_Using_Command_And_DataAdapter(ByVal cnstr As String, ByVal strQuery As String)

    Dim cmd As New System.Data.OleDb.OleDbCommand()
    cmd.Connection = New System.Data.OleDb.OleDbConnection
    cmd.Connection.ConnectionString = cnstr
    cmd.Connection.Open()
    cmd.CommandType = System.Data.CommandType.Text
    cmd.ExecuteNonQuery()

    da = New OleDbDataAdapter(cmd)

End Sub
Public Sub create_OleDb_Connection_Using_The_DataAdapter(ByVal cnstr As String, ByVal strQuery As String)

    da = New OleDbDataAdapter(strQuery, cnstr)

End Sub

Public Sub create_OleDb_Connection_Using_Connection_Command_And_DataReader(ByVal cnstr As String, ByVal strQuery As String)


    Dim cn As OleDbConnection = New OleDbConnection
    cn.ConnectionString = cnstr
    cn.Open()

    Dim cmd As OleDbCommand = New OleDbCommand()
    cmd.Connection = cn
    cmd.CommandType = System.Data.CommandType.Text
    drr = cmd.ExecuteReader()

End Sub

Public Sub create_OleDb_Connection_Using_Command_And_DataReader(ByVal cnstr As String, ByVal strQuery As String)

    Dim cmd As New System.Data.OleDb.OleDbCommand()
    cmd.Connection = New System.Data.OleDb.OleDbConnection
    cmd.Connection.ConnectionString = cnstr
    cmd.Connection.Open()
    cmd.CommandType = System.Data.CommandType.Text
    drr = cmd.ExecuteReader()

End Sub
```

In the next chapter, we will add the finishing touches to this module.

Adding The Population of the DataSet, DataTable and DataView

Using the DataAdapter

Adding the functionality of returning a DataSet, DataTable, and DataView is pretty straight forward and, perhaps the easiest to do.

The primary thing to remember is you must first prepare the OleDbDataAdapter first – meaning you must first use one of the examples in the previous chapter first before using one of the routines below.

```
Public Function Populate_The_DataSet(Optional ByVal tablename As String = "") As System.Data.DataSet
    Dim ds As New DataSet
    If tablename <> "" Then
        da.Fill(ds, tablename)
    Else
        da.Fill(ds)
```

```vb
        End If

        Return ds

    End Function

    Public Function Populate_The_DataTable(Optional ByVal tablename As String = "") As System.Data.DataTable

        Dim dt As New DataTable
        If tablename <> "" Then

            da.Fill(dt)
            dt.TableName = tablename

        Else

            da.Fill(dt)

        End If

        Return dt

    End Function

    Public Function Populate_The_DataView(Optional ByVal tablename As String = "") As System.Data.DataView

        Dim dt As New DataTable
        If tablename <> "" Then

            da.Fill(dt)
            dt.TableName = tablename

        Else

            da.Fill(dt)

        End If

        Return dt.DefaultView

    End Function

End Module
```

Okay, so we now have a module that can be used to produce a dataset, datatable, dataview or a datareader. How do we use this to create a report?

Working with IEnumerable Collections

Dynamic driving the reports

Here's a couple of key words for you. Bound = DataSource, Dynamic = DataBindings. If you have worked with Windows Presentation Foundation (WPF) application, you know what is meant when you use the DataContext and it only accepts a DataView.

If you haven't then you really need to see what I am talking about because the ReportViewer control works similar to the way the WPF binding engine works.

Here's the xml:

```
<Window x:Class="MainWindow"
    xmlns="http://schemas.microsoft.com/winfx/2006/xaml/presentation"
    xmlns:x="http://schemas.microsoft.com/winfx/2006/xaml"
    Title="MainWindow" Height="350" Width="525">
    <Grid>
        <DataGrid AutoGenerateColumns="true" Height= "Auto" HorizontalAlignment="Stretch"
Margin="0,0,0,0" Name="DataGrid1" VerticalAlignment="Stretch" Width="Auto"
ItemsSource="{Binding}"/>
    </Grid>
</Window>
```

Here's the code:

```
Dim rs As Object = CreateObject("ADODB.Recordset")
rs.ActiveConnection = "Provider=Microsoft.Jet.OleDb.4.0;Data Source=C:\nwind.mdb"
rs.CursorLocation = 3
rs.Locktype = 3
rs.Source = "Select * from Products"
rs.Open()
```

```
Dim ds As New System.Data.DataSet
Dim da As New System.Data.OleDb.OleDbDataAdapter
da.Fill(ds, rs, "Products")

DataGrid1.DataContext = ds.Tables(0).DefaultView
```
Here's the results:

ProductID	ProductName	SupplierID	CategoryID	QuantityPerUnit	UnitPrice	UnitsInStock	UnitsOnOrder	ReorderLevel	Discontinued
1	Chai	1	1	10 boxes x 20 bags	18	39	0	10	☐
2	Chang	1	1	24 - 12 oz bottles	19	17	40	25	☐
3	Aniseed Syrup	1	2	12 - 550 ml bottles	10	13	70	25	☐
4	Chef Anton's Cajun Seasoning	2	2	48 - 6 oz jars	22	53	0	0	☐
5	Chef Anton's Gumbo Mix	2	2	36 boxes	21.35	0	0	0	☑
6	Grandma's Boysenberry Spread	3	2	12 - 8 oz jars	25	120	0	25	☐
7	Uncle Bob's Organic Dried Pears	3	7	12 - 1 lb pkgs.	30	15	0	10	☐
8	Northwoods Cranberry Sauce	3	2	12 - 12 oz jars	40	6	0	0	☐
9	Mishi Kobe Niku	4	6	18 - 500 g pkgs.	97	29	0	0	☑
10	Ikura	4	8	12 - 200 ml jars	31	31	0	0	☐
11	Queso Cabrales	5	4	1 kg pkg.	21	22	30	30	☐
12	Queso Manchego La Pastora	5	4	10 - 500 g pkgs.	38	86	0	0	☐
13	Konbu	6	8	2 kg box	6	24	0	5	☐
14	Tofu	6	7	40 - 100 g pkgs.	23.25	35	0	0	☐

As you can see the DataGrid is bound as it has checkmarks instead of the true or false in the discontinued field.

You can also use the DataTable and use its default view to do the same thing:

```
Dim rs As Object = CreateObject("ADODB.Recordset")
rs.ActiveConnection = "Provider=Microsoft.Jet.OleDb.4.0;Data Source=C:\nwind.mdb"
rs.CursorLocation = 3
rs.Locktype = 3
rs.Source = "Select * from Products"
rs.Open()

Dim dt As New System.Data.DataTable
Dim da As New System.Data.OleDb.OleDbDataAdapter
da.Fill(dt, rs)
dt.TableName = "Products"
DataGrid1.DataContext = dt.DefaultView
```

Here's a Report that was created by first creating a DataSource and selecting the table: Products. After that, I used the Report Wizard to bind the report with the DataSource.

The solution looks completely different then what we've already worked with:

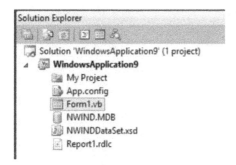

Solution Explorer

Solution 'WindowsApplication9' (1 project)
- **WindowsApplication9**
  - My Project
  - App.config
  - Form1.vb
  - NWIND.MDB
  - NWINDDataSet.xsd
  - Report1.rdlc

And no code was required. The difference between the two applications has some profound advantages and disadvantages.

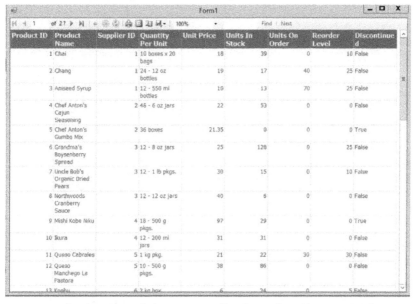

Product ID	Product Name	Supplier ID	Quantity Per Unit	Unit Price	Units In Stock	Units On Order	Reorder Level	Discontinued
1	Chai	1	10 boxes x 20 bags	18	39	0	10	False
2	Chang	1	24 - 12 oz bottles	19	17	40	25	False
3	Aniseed Syrup	1	12 - 550 ml bottles	10	13	70	25	False
4	Chef Anton's Cajun Seasoning	2	46 - 6 oz jars	22	53	0	0	False
5	Chef Anton's Gumbo Mix	2	36 boxes	21.35	0	0	0	True
6	Grandma's Boysenberry Spread	3	12 - 8 oz jars	25	120	0	25	False
7	Uncle Bob's Organic Dried Pears	3	12 - 1 lb pkgs.	30	15	0	10	False
8	Northwoods Cranberry Sauce	3	12 - 12 oz jars	40	6	0	0	False
9	Mishi Kobe Niku	4	18 - 500 g pkgs.	97	29	0	0	True
10	Ikura	4	12 - 200 ml jars	31	31	0	0	False
11	Queso Cabrales	5	1 kg pkg.	21	22	30	30	False
12	Queso Manchego La Pastora	5	10 - 500 g pkgs.	38	86	0	0	False
13	Konbu	6	2 kg box	6	24	0	5	False

Now, in the case of the WPF Application, what if we wanted to create the information in the DataGridView dynamically?

```
Public Structure Products
    Public Property ProductID As String
    Public Property ProductName As String
    Public Property SupplierID As String
    Public Property CategoryID As String
    Public Property QuantityPerUnit As String
    Public Property UnitPrice As String
    Public Property UnitsInStock As String
    Public Property UnitsOnOrder As String
    Public Property ReorderLevel As String
    Public Property Discontinued As String
End Structure
```

```vb
    Dim mcHammer As System.Collections.ObjectModel.ObservableCollection(Of Products) = New
System.Collections.ObjectModel.ObservableCollection(Of Products)

    Private Sub Window__Loaded(ByVal sender As System.Object, ByVal e As System.Windows.RoutedEventArgs)
Handles MyBase.Loaded

        Dim db As Binding
        Dim tc As DataGridTextColumn

        db = New Binding("ProductID")
        tc = New DataGridTextColumn()
        tc.Header = "ProductID"
        tc.Binding = db
        DataGrid1.Columns.Add(tc)

        db = New Binding("ProductName")
        tc = New DataGridTextColumn()
        tc.Header = "ProductName"
        tc.Binding = db
        DataGrid1.Columns.Add(tc)

        db = New Binding("SupplierID")
        tc = New DataGridTextColumn()
        tc.Header = "SupplierID"
        tc.Binding = db
        DataGrid1.Columns.Add(tc)

        db = New Binding("CategoryID")
        tc = New DataGridTextColumn()
        tc.Header = "CategoryID"
        tc.Binding = db
        DataGrid1.Columns.Add(tc)

        db = New Binding("QuantityPerUnit")
        tc = New DataGridTextColumn()
        tc.Header = "QuantityPerUnit"
        tc.Binding = db
        DataGrid1.Columns.Add(tc)

        db = New Binding("UnitPrice")
        tc = New DataGridTextColumn()
        tc.Header = "UnitPrice"
        tc.Binding = db
        DataGrid1.Columns.Add(tc)

        db = New Binding("UnitsInStock")
        tc = New DataGridTextColumn()
        tc.Header = "UnitsInStock"
        tc.Binding = db
        DataGrid1.Columns.Add(tc)

        db = New Binding("UnitsOnOrder")
        tc = New DataGridTextColumn()
        tc.Header = "UnitsOnOrder"
        tc.Binding = db
        DataGrid1.Columns.Add(tc)

        db = New Binding("ReorderLevel")
        tc = New DataGridTextColumn()
        tc.Header = "ReorderLevel"
        tc.Binding = db
        DataGrid1.Columns.Add(tc)

        db = New Binding("Discontinued")
        tc = New DataGridTextColumn()
        tc.Header = "Discontinued"
```

```
tc.Binding = db
DataGrid1.Columns.Add(tc)

Dim rs As Object = CreateObject("ADODB.Recordset")
rs.ActiveConnection = "Provider=Microsoft.Jet.OleDb.4.0;Data Source=C:\nwind.mdb"
rs.CursorLocation = 3
rs.Locktype = 3
rs.Source = "Select * from Products"
rs.Open()

rs.MoveLast()
rs.MoveFirst()


Do While Not rs.EOF
    Dim myProducts As New Products
    For x As Integer = 0 To rs.Fields.Count - 1
        myProducts.ProductID = rs.Fields("ProductID").Value
        myProducts.ProductName = rs.Fields("ProductName").Value
        myProducts.SupplierID = rs.Fields("SupplierID").Value
        myProducts.CategoryID = rs.Fields("CategoryID").Value
        myProducts.QuantityPerUnit = rs.Fields("QuantityPerUnit").Value
        myProducts.UnitPrice = rs.Fields("UnitPrice").Value
        myProducts.UnitsInStock = rs.Fields("UnitsInStock").Value
        myProducts.UnitsOnOrder = rs.Fields("UnitsOnOrder").Value
        myProducts.ReorderLevel = rs.Fields("ReorderLevel").Value
        myProducts.Discontinued = rs.Fields("Discontinued").Value
    Next
    mcHammer.Add(myProducts)
    rs.MoveNext()
Loop

DataGrid1.ItemsSource = mcHammer

End Sub
```

And this creates:

ProductID	ProductName	SupplierID	CategoryID	QuantityPerUnit	UnitPrice	UnitsInStock	UnitsOnOrder	ReorderLevel	Discontinue
1	Chai	1	1	10 boxes x 20 bags	18	39	0	10	False
2	Chang	1	1	24 - 12 oz bottles	19	17	40	25	False
3	Aniseed Syrup	1	2	12 - 550 ml bottles	10	13	70	25	False
4	Chef Anton's Cajun Seasoning	2	2	48 - 6 oz jars	22	53	0	0	False
5	Chef Anton's Gumbo Mix	2	2	36 boxes	21.35	0	0	0	True
6	Grandma's Boysenberry Spread	3	2	12 - 8 oz jars	25	120	0	25	False
7	Uncle Bob's Organic Dried Pears	3	7	12 - 1 lb pkgs.	30	15	0	10	False
8	Northwoods Cranberry Sauce	3	2	12 - 12 oz jars	40	6	0	0	False
9	Mishi Kobe Niku	4	6	18 - 500 g pkgs.	97	29	0	0	True
10	Ikura	4	8	12 - 200 ml jars	31	31	0	0	False
11	Queso Cabrales	5	4	1 kg pkg.	21	22	30	30	False
12	Queso Manchego La Pastora	5	4	10 - 500 g pkgs.	38	86	0	0	False
13	Konbu	6	8	2 kg box	6	24	0	5	False
14	Tofu	6	7	40 - 100 g pkgs.	23.25	35	0	0	False
15	Genen Shouyu	6	2	24 - 250 ml bottles	15.5	39	0	5	False
16	Pavlova	7	3	32 - 500 g boxes	17.45	29	0	10	False
17	Alice Mutton	7	6	20 - 1 kg tins	39	0	0	0	True
18	Carnarvon Tigers	7	8	16 kg pkg.	62.5	42	0	0	False
19	Teatime Chocolate Biscuits	8	3	10 boxes x 12 pieces	9.2	25	0	5	False

What I used was an IEnumerable Collection. The same code was used – with a few modifications:

```vbnet
Public Class Form2
    Public Structure Products
        Public Property ProductID As String
        Public Property ProductName As String
        Public Property SupplierID As String
        Public Property CategoryID As String
        Public Property QuantityPerUnit As String
        Public Property UnitPrice As String
        Public Property UnitsInStock As String
        Public Property UnitsOnOrder As String
        Public Property ReorderLevel As String
        Public Property Discontinued As String
    End Structure
    Public mcHammer As System.Collections.ObjectModel.ObservableCollection(Of Products) = New
System.Collections.ObjectModel.ObservableCollection(Of Products)
    Public Ds As DataSet
    Private Sub Form2_Load(ByVal sender As System.Object, ByVal e As System.EventArgs) Handles MyBase.Load

        Dim rs As Object = CreateObject("ADODB.Recordset")
        rs.ActiveConnection = "Provider=Microsoft.Jet.OleDb.4.0;Data Source=C:\nwind.mdb"
        rs.CursorLocation = 3
        rs.Locktype = 3
        rs.Source = "Select * from Products"
        rs.Open()

        rs.MoveLast()
        rs.MoveFirst()


        Do While Not rs.EOF
            Dim myProducts As New Products
            For x As Integer = 0 To rs.Fields.Count - 1
                myProducts.ProductID = rs.Fields("ProductID").Value
                myProducts.ProductName = rs.Fields("ProductName").Value
                myProducts.SupplierID = rs.Fields("SupplierID").Value
                myProducts.CategoryID = rs.Fields("CategoryID").Value
                myProducts.QuantityPerUnit = rs.Fields("QuantityPerUnit").Value
                myProducts.UnitPrice = rs.Fields("UnitPrice").Value
                myProducts.UnitsInStock = rs.Fields("UnitsInStock").Value
                myProducts.UnitsOnOrder = rs.Fields("UnitsOnOrder").Value
                myProducts.ReorderLevel = rs.Fields("ReorderLevel").Value
                myProducts.Discontinued = rs.Fields("Discontinued").Value
            Next
            mcHammer.Add(myProducts)
            rs.MoveNext()
        Loop

        ReportViewer1.LocalReport.DataSources.Clear()
        ReportViewer1.LocalReport.DataSources.Add(New
Microsoft.Reporting.WinForms.ReportDataSource("DataSet1", mcHammer))
        Me.ReportViewer1.RefreshReport()

    End Sub
```

Produced this:

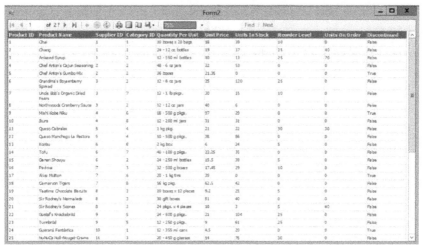

Here's the two forms view that uses the Collections:

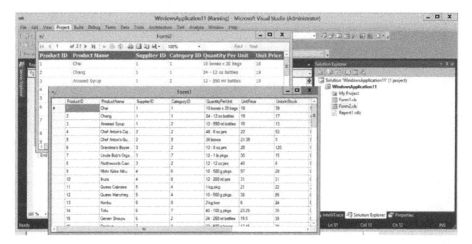

No datasets, no xsd, and no xml needed to build the values the ReportViewer needs to use to display the values. Just some good old hey wait a minute logic that worked!

Now, you're probably wondering, if this is that easy to work with, why isn't there more documentation on working with all of these different ways to create these reports?

That's a good question worthy of being a book in itself. I have 65 pages I need to fill with quality information. Up to this point, I have pretty much given you a world wind tour on how to create these reports. And I think it is time to go from whirl wind to a very detailed approach and discuss how to automate each way we just covered to make all of this work exactly the way you need it to work.

Building the routines that create the IEnumerable reports
Let the computer do the work for you

Using a structure or a class that has all of the properties in it are two universal ways to create the backbone of your reports. But they are time consuming and are used two times.

Once when that kind of structure or class needs to be built and, again, when the structure or class needs to be referenced and populated with property values. Okay, that sounds good but what are these structures and classes really doing?

They are creating a row or definition table that defines how a columns of information should be handled. The problem is, as long as the structure or class contains three columns in them, they don't require a lot of time to build. Past that, you really need to consider automating the process. And that is where we need to create a program that writes programs.

Let's take a look at this structure:

```
Public Structure Products
    Public Property ProductID As String
    Public Property ProductName As String
    Public Property SupplierID As String
    Public Property CategoryID As String
    Public Property QuantityPerUnit As String
    Public Property UnitPrice As String
    Public Property UnitsInStock As String
    Public Property UnitsOnOrder As String
    Public Property ReorderLevel As String
    Public Property Discontinued As String
End Structure
```

It contains ten properties all defined as strings. It isn't an accurate definition of what each System Type each really is. Using a string just made it simpler to write and use.

Looking at the same fields using the OleDbDataAdapter and a DataTable will help use to have a better understanding regarding what each data type each really is and how each should be data typed.

This code below does exactly that:

```
Dim da As New OleDb.OleDbDataAdapter("Select * from Products",
"Provider=Microsoft.Jet.OleDb.4.0;Data Source=C:\nwind.mdb")
    Dim dt As New DataTable
    da.Fill(dt)
    Debug.Print("   Public Structure Products")
    For Each Col As DataColumn In dt.Columns
        Debug.Print("      Public Property " & Col.Caption & " As " & Col.DataType.ToString())
    Next
    Debug.Print("   End Structure")
```

And produces this:

```
    Public Structure Products
        Public Property ProductID As System.Int32
        Public Property ProductName As System.String
        Public Property SupplierID As System.Int32
        Public Property CategoryID As System.Int32
        Public Property QuantityPerUnit As System.String
        Public Property UnitPrice As System.Decimal
        Public Property UnitsInStock As System.Int16
        Public Property UnitsOnOrder As System.Int16
        Public Property ReorderLevel As System.Int16
        Public Property Discontinued As System.Boolean
    End Structure
```

It took the computer less than a second to build.

Now, the question here is, while it took you on a split second to build, it also took you time to write the program needed to produce it. And you would be right. Until you make it totally dynamic and reusable code:

```
Public Sub Create_The_Structure(ByVal cnstr As String, ByVal strQuery As String, ByVal TableName As String)

    Dim da As New OleDb.OleDbDataAdapter(strQuery, cnstr)
    Dim dt As New DataTable
    da.Fill(dt)
    Debug.Print("   Public Structure " & TableName)
    For Each Col As DataColumn In dt.Columns
        Debug.Print("      Public Property " & Col.Caption & " As " & Col.DataType.ToString())
    Next
    Debug.Print("   End Structure")

End Sub
```

Now that we know how to create the structure, what do we do with it?

Well, first, we need to create an ObservableCollection that with be our row collection resource:

```
Public mcHammer As System.Collections.ObjectModel.ObservableCollection(Of Products) = New
System.Collections.ObjectModel.ObservableCollection(Of Products)
```

Then we need to make a reference to our row – structure that we will use to populate the properties in each row and then add the row to the collection.

```
Dim da As New OleDb.OleDbDataAdapter("Select * from Products", "Provider=Microsoft.Jet.OleDb.4.0;Data
Source=C:\nwind.mdb")
Dim dt As New DataTable
da.Fill(dt)

Debug.Print("    For each row as DataRow in dt.Rows")
Debug.Print("        Dim myproducts as new products")
For Each Col As DataColumn In dt.Columns
    Debug.Print("        myproducts." & Col.Caption & " = row.Item("""" & Col.Caption & """")")
Next
Debug.Print("        mcHammer.Add(myproducts)")
Debug.Print("    Next")
```

Which produces this:

```
For each row as datarow in dt.Rows
    Dim myproducts as new products
    myproducts.ProductID = row.Item("ProductID")
    myproducts.ProductName = row.Item("ProductName")
    myproducts.SupplierID = row.Item("SupplierID")
    myproducts.CategoryID = row.Item("CategoryID")
    myproducts.QuantityPerUnit = row.Item("QuantityPerUnit")
    myproducts.UnitPrice = row.Item("UnitPrice")
    myproducts.UnitsInStock = row.Item("UnitsInStock")
    myproducts.UnitsOnOrder = row.Item("UnitsOnOrder")
    myproducts.ReorderLevel = row.Item("ReorderLevel")
    myproducts.Discontinued = row.Item("Discontinued")
    mcHammer.Add(myproducts)
Next
```

When combined, it creates this:

```
Public Class Form2
    Public Structure Products
        Public Property ProductID As System.Int32
        Public Property ProductName As System.String
        Public Property SupplierID As System.Int32
        Public Property CategoryID As System.Int32
        Public Property QuantityPerUnit As System.String
        Public Property UnitPrice As System.Decimal
        Public Property UnitsInStock As System.Int16
        Public Property UnitsOnOrder As System.Int16
        Public Property ReorderLevel As System.Int16
        Public Property Discontinued As System.Boolean
    End Structure
```

```vb
Public mcHammer As System.Collections.ObjectModel.ObservableCollection(Of Products) = New
System.Collections.ObjectModel.ObservableCollection(Of Products)
Public Ds As DataSet
Private Sub Form2_Load(ByVal sender As System.Object, ByVal e As System.EventArgs) Handles MyBase.Load

    Dim da As OleDb.OleDbDataAdapter = New OleDb.OleDbDataAdapter("Select * from Products", _
"Provider=Microsoft.Jet.OleDb.4.0;Data Source=C:\nwind.mdb")
    Dim dt As New DataTable
    da.Fill(dt)
    dt.TableName = "Products"

    For Each row As DataRow In dt.Rows
        Dim myproducts As New Products
        myproducts.ProductID = row.Item("ProductID")
        myproducts.ProductName = row.Item("ProductName")
        myproducts.SupplierID = row.Item("SupplierID")
        myproducts.CategoryID = row.Item("CategoryID")
        myproducts.QuantityPerUnit = row.Item("QuantityPerUnit")
        myproducts.UnitPrice = row.Item("UnitPrice")
        myproducts.UnitsInStock = row.Item("UnitsInStock")
        myproducts.UnitsOnOrder = row.Item("UnitsOnOrder")
        myproducts.ReorderLevel = row.Item("ReorderLevel")
        myproducts.Discontinued = row.Item("Discontinued")
        mcHammer.Add(myproducts)
    Next


    ReportViewer1.LocalReport.DataSources.Clear()
    ReportViewer1.LocalReport.DataSources.Add(New _
Microsoft.Reporting.WinForms.ReportDataSource("DataSet1", mcHammer))
    Me.ReportViewer1.RefreshReport()

End Sub
End Class
```

Which produces this:

Product ID	Product Name	Supplier ID	Category ID	Quantity Per Unit	Unit Price	Units In Stock	Reorder Level	Units On Order	Discontinued
1	Chai	1	1	10 boxes x 20 bags	18	39	10	0	False
2	Chang	1	1	24 - 12 oz bottles	19	17	25	40	False
3	Aniseed Syrup	1	2	12 - 550 ml bottles	10	13	25	70	False
4	Chef Anton's Cajun Seasoning	2	2	48 - 6 oz jars	22	53	0	0	False
5	Chef Anton's Gumbo Mix	2	2	36 boxes	21.35	0	0	0	True
6	Grandma's Boysenberry Spread	3	2	12 - 8 oz jars	25	120	25	0	False
7	Uncle Bob's Organic Dried Pears	3	7	12 - 1 lb pkgs.	30	15	10	0	False
8	Northwoods Cranberry Sauce	3	2	12 - 12 oz jars	40	6	0	0	False
9	Mishi Kobe Niku	4	6	18 - 500 g pkgs.	97	29	0	0	True
10	Ikura	4	8	12 - 200 ml jars	31	31	0	0	False
11	Queso Cabrales	5	4	1 kg pkg.	21	22	30	30	False
12	Queso Manchego La Pastora	5	4	10 - 500 g pkgs.	38	86	0	0	False
13	Konbu	6	8	2 kg box	6	24	5	0	False
14	Tofu	6	7	40 - 100 g pkgs.	23.25	35	0	0	False
15	Genen Shouyu	6	2	24 - 250 ml bottles	15.5	39	5	0	False
16	Pavlova	7	3	32 - 500 g boxes	17.45	29	10	0	False
17	Alice Mutton	7	6	20 - 1 kg tins	39	0	0	0	True
18	Carnarvon Tigers	7	8	16 kg pkg.	62.5	42	0	0	False
19	Teatime Chocolate Biscuits	8	3	10 boxes x 12 pieces	9.2	25	5	0	False
20	Sir Rodney's Marmalade	8	3	30 gift boxes	81	40	0	0	False
21	Sir Rodney's Scones	8	3	24 pkgs. x 4 pieces	10	3	5	40	False
22	Gustaf's Knäckebröd	9	5	24 - 500 g pkgs.	21	104	25	0	False
23	Tunnbröd	9	5	12 - 250 g pkgs.	9	61	25	0	False

There is, of course, one piece of this puzzle we haven't automated and that is the actual report file itself, which, believe it or not is pretty easy to generate dynamically.

The first thing I'm going to do is create an Excel spreadsheet filled with information on Services. Three sheets will be created. One for all the all services installed, one for all the running services and one for all the stopped services.

Then we're going to take Excel spreadsheet, use OleDb and produce three reports.

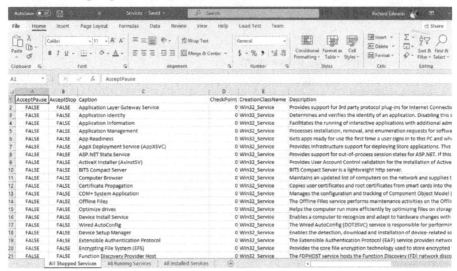

Now that we have the spreadsheet, we're going to use the Microsoft.ACE.OleDbProvider along with the Excel 8.0 ISAM

Here's the code to create the spreadsheets:

```
Public ns() As String = Nothing
Public l() As Integer

Function GetValue(ByVal Name, ByVal obj)
    Dim tempstr, pos, pName
    pName = Name
    tempstr = obj.GetObjectText_
    Name = Name + " = "
    pos = InStr(tempstr, Name)
    If pos Then
        pos = pos + Len(Name)
        tempstr = Mid(tempstr, pos, Len(tempstr))
        pos = InStr(tempstr, ";")
        tempstr = Mid(tempstr, 1, pos - 1)
        tempstr = Replace(tempstr, Chr(34), "")
        tempstr = Replace(tempstr, "{", "")
        tempstr = Replace(tempstr, "}", "")
        tempstr = Trim(tempstr)
        If obj.Properties_(pName).CIMType = 101 Then
            tempstr = Mid(tempstr, 5, 2) + "/" + _
                Mid(tempstr, 7, 2) + "/" + _
                Mid(tempstr, 1, 4) + " " + _
```

```vb
                Mid(tempstr, 9, 2) + ":" + _
                Mid(tempstr, 11, 2) + ":" + _
                Mid(tempstr, 11, 2) + ":" + _
                Mid(tempstr, 13, 2)
        End If
        GetValue = tempstr
    Else
        GetValue = ""
    End If

End Function


Public Sub CREATE_THE_EXCEL_SPREADSHEET()

    Dim oexcel As Object = CreateObject("Excel.Application")
    oexcel.Visible = True
    Dim wb As Object = oexcel.Workbooks.Add()

    Dim ws1 As Object = wb.Worksheets(1)
    ws1.Name = "All Installed Services"

    Dim ws2 As Object = wb.Worksheets.Add()
    ws2.Name = "All Running Services"

    Dim ws3 As Object = wb.Worksheets.Add()
    ws3.Name = "All Stopped Services"

    Dim objs As Object = GetObject("Winmgmts:\\.\root\cimv2").InstancesOf("Win32_Service")

    Dim a As Integer = 0
    Dim b As Integer = 0
    Dim c As Integer = 0

    Dim x As Integer = 0

    For Each obj In objs
        ReDim ns(obj.Properties_.Count - 1)
        ReDim l(obj.Properties_.Count - 1)
        For Each prop In obj.Properties_
            ns(x) = prop.Name
            l(x) = prop.Name.ToString().Length

            ws1.Cells(1, x + 1) = prop.name
            ws2.Cells(1, x + 1) = prop.name
            ws3.Cells(1, x + 1) = prop.name
            x = x + 1
        Next

        Exit For

    Next

    x = 0

    For Each obj In objs

        For Each n As String In ns

            ws1.Cells(a + 2, x + 1) = GetValue(n, obj)

            Select Case obj.State

                Case "Running"
```

```vbnet
            ws2.Cells(b + 2, x + 1) = GetValue(n, obj)

        Case "Stopped"

            ws3.Cells(c + 2, x + 1) = GetValue(n, obj)

    End Select
      x = x + 1
    Next
    x = 0

    Select Case obj.State

        Case "Running"

            b = b + 1

        Case "Stopped"

            c = c + 1

    End Select
      a = a + 1

  Next

  For y As Integer = 0 To ns.GetLength(0) - 1

      ws1.Columns(y + 1).AutoFit()
      ws2.Columns(y + 1).AutoFit()
      ws3.Columns(y + 1).AutoFit()

  Next

End Sub

Public Sub Get_Excel_Column_Widths()


  Dim oexcel As Object = CreateObject("Excel.Application")
  oexcel.Visible = True
  Dim wb As Object = oexcel.Workbooks.Add("C:\Services.xlsx")
  Dim ws1 As Object = wb.Worksheets(1)
  For x As Integer = 0 To ns.GetLength(0) - 1
     l(x) = ws1.Columns(x + 1).Width
  Next

End Sub
```

Here's the code to create the reports dynamically:


```vbnet
Public Sub Create_THE_RDLC_FILE(ByVal RName As String)


  Dim fso As Object = CreateObject("Scripting.FileSystemObject")
  Dim txtstream As Object = fso.OpenTextFile(Application.StartupPath & "\" & RName & ".rdlc", 2, True, -2)
  txtstream.WriteLine("<?xml version=""1.0""?>")
```

```vb
txtstream.WriteLine("<Report
xmlns:rd="""http://schemas.microsoft.com/SQLServer/reporting/reportdesigner""
xmlns="""http://schemas.microsoft.com/sqlserver/reporting/2008/01/reportdefinition""">")
txtstream.WriteLine("  <DataSources>")
txtstream.WriteLine("    <DataSource Name="""WindowsApplication5""">")
txtstream.WriteLine("      <ConnectionProperties>")
txtstream.WriteLine("        <DataProvider>System.Data.DataSet</DataProvider>")
txtstream.WriteLine("        <ConnectString>/* Local Connection */</ConnectString>")
txtstream.WriteLine("      </ConnectionProperties>")
txtstream.WriteLine("      <rd:DataSourceID>4ada475a-519d-4774-8a8e-
cd804357bc15</rd:DataSourceID>")
txtstream.WriteLine("    </DataSource>")
txtstream.WriteLine("  </DataSources>")
txtstream.WriteLine("  <DataSets>")
txtstream.WriteLine("    <DataSet Name="""DataSet1""">")
txtstream.WriteLine("      <Fields>")

For x As Integer = 0 To ns.Count - 1

    txtstream.WriteLine("        <Field Name=""" & ns(x) & """>")
    txtstream.WriteLine("          <DataField>" & ns(x) & "</DataField>")
    txtstream.WriteLine("          <rd:TypeName>System.String</rd:TypeName>")
    txtstream.WriteLine("        </Field>")

Next

txtstream.WriteLine("      </Fields>")
txtstream.WriteLine("      <Query>")
txtstream.WriteLine("        <DataSourceName>WindowsApplication5</DataSourceName>")
txtstream.WriteLine("        <CommandText>/* Local Query */</CommandText>")
txtstream.WriteLine("      </Query>")
txtstream.WriteLine("      <rd:DataSetInfo>")
txtstream.WriteLine("        <rd:DataSetName>WindowsApplication5</rd:DataSetName>")
txtstream.WriteLine("        <rd:TableName>data</rd:TableName>")
txtstream.WriteLine("
<rd:ObjectDataSourceSelectMethod>win32_bios</rd:ObjectDataSourceSelectMethod>")
txtstream.WriteLine("        <rd:ObjectDataSourceType>WindowsApplication5.data, win32_bios.Designer.vb,
Version=0.0.0.0, Culture=neutral, PublicKeyToken=null</rd:ObjectDataSourceType>")
txtstream.WriteLine("      </rd:DataSetInfo>")
txtstream.WriteLine("    </DataSet>")
txtstream.WriteLine("  </DataSets>")
txtstream.WriteLine("  <Body>")
txtstream.WriteLine("    <ReportItems>")
txtstream.WriteLine("      <Tablix Name="""Tablix1""">")
txtstream.WriteLine("        <TablixBody>")
txtstream.WriteLine("          <TablixColumns>")

For x As Integer = 0 To ns.Count - 1

    txtstream.WriteLine("            <TablixColumn>")
    txtstream.WriteLine("              <Width>" & l(x) / 47 & "in</Width>")
    txtstream.WriteLine("            </TablixColumn>")

Next

txtstream.WriteLine("          </TablixColumns>")
txtstream.WriteLine("          <TablixRows>")
txtstream.WriteLine("            <TablixRow>")
txtstream.WriteLine("              <Height>0.25in</Height>")
txtstream.WriteLine("              <TablixCells>")

For x As Integer = 0 To ns.Count - 1

    txtstream.WriteLine("                <TablixCell>")
    txtstream.WriteLine("                  <CellContents>")
    txtstream.WriteLine("                    <Textbox Name="""Textbox" & x + 1 & """>")
```

```vbnet
txtstream.WriteLine("            <CanGrow>true</CanGrow>")
txtstream.WriteLine("            <KeepTogether>true</KeepTogether>")
txtstream.WriteLine("            <Paragraphs>")
txtstream.WriteLine("             <Paragraph>")
txtstream.WriteLine("              <TextRuns>")
txtstream.WriteLine("               <TextRun>")
txtstream.WriteLine("                <Value>" & ns(x) & "</Value>")
txtstream.WriteLine("                <Style>")
txtstream.WriteLine("                 <FontFamily>Tahoma</FontFamily>")
txtstream.WriteLine("                 <FontSize>11pt</FontSize>")
txtstream.WriteLine("                 <FontWeight>Bold</FontWeight>")
txtstream.WriteLine("                 <Color>White</Color>")
txtstream.WriteLine("                </Style>")
txtstream.WriteLine("               </TextRun>")
txtstream.WriteLine("              </TextRuns>")
txtstream.WriteLine("              <Style />")
txtstream.WriteLine("             </Paragraph>")
txtstream.WriteLine("            </Paragraphs>")
txtstream.WriteLine("            <rd:DefaultName>Textbox" & x + 1 & "</rd:DefaultName>")
txtstream.WriteLine("            <Style>")
txtstream.WriteLine("             <Border>")
txtstream.WriteLine("              <Color>#7292cc</Color>")
txtstream.WriteLine("              <Style>Solid</Style>")
txtstream.WriteLine("             </Border>")
txtstream.WriteLine("             <BackgroundColor>#4c68a2</BackgroundColor>")
txtstream.WriteLine("             <PaddingLeft>2pt</PaddingLeft>")
txtstream.WriteLine("             <PaddingRight>2pt</PaddingRight>")
txtstream.WriteLine("             <PaddingTop>2pt</PaddingTop>")
txtstream.WriteLine("             <PaddingBottom>2pt</PaddingBottom>")
txtstream.WriteLine("            </Style>")
txtstream.WriteLine("           </Textbox>")
txtstream.WriteLine("          </CellContents>")
txtstream.WriteLine("         </TablixCell>")

Next


txtstream.WriteLine("        </TablixCells>")
txtstream.WriteLine("       </TablixRow>")
txtstream.WriteLine("       <TablixRow>")
txtstream.WriteLine("        <Height>0.25in</Height>")
txtstream.WriteLine("        <TablixCells>")

For x As Integer = 0 To ns.Count - 1

txtstream.WriteLine("         <TablixCell>")
txtstream.WriteLine("          <CellContents>")
txtstream.WriteLine("           <Textbox Name=""" & ns(x) & """>")
txtstream.WriteLine("            <CanGrow>true</CanGrow>")
txtstream.WriteLine("            <KeepTogether>true</KeepTogether>")
txtstream.WriteLine("            <Paragraphs>")
txtstream.WriteLine("             <Paragraph>")
txtstream.WriteLine("              <TextRuns>")
txtstream.WriteLine("               <TextRun>")
txtstream.WriteLine("                <Value>=Fields!" & ns(x) & ".Value</Value>")
txtstream.WriteLine("                <Style>")
txtstream.WriteLine("                 <FontFamily>Tahoma</FontFamily>")
txtstream.WriteLine("                 <Color>#4d4d4d</Color>")
txtstream.WriteLine("                </Style>")
txtstream.WriteLine("               </TextRun>")
txtstream.WriteLine("              </TextRuns>")
txtstream.WriteLine("              <Style />")
txtstream.WriteLine("             </Paragraph>")
txtstream.WriteLine("            </Paragraphs>")
txtstream.WriteLine("            <rd:DefaultName>" & ns(x) & "</rd:DefaultName>")
txtstream.WriteLine("            <Style>")
```

```vb
        txtstream.WriteLine("                    <Border>")
        txtstream.WriteLine("                      <Color>#e5e5e5</Color>")
        txtstream.WriteLine("                      <Style>Solid</Style>")
        txtstream.WriteLine("                    </Border>")
        txtstream.WriteLine("                    <PaddingLeft>2pt</PaddingLeft>")
        txtstream.WriteLine("                    <PaddingRight>2pt</PaddingRight>")
        txtstream.WriteLine("                    <PaddingTop>2pt</PaddingTop>")
        txtstream.WriteLine("                    <PaddingBottom>2pt</PaddingBottom>")
        txtstream.WriteLine("                  </Style>")
        txtstream.WriteLine("                </Textbox>")
        txtstream.WriteLine("              </CellContents>")
        txtstream.WriteLine("            </TablixCell>")

Next

    txtstream.WriteLine("          </TablixCells>")
    txtstream.WriteLine("        </TablixRow>")
    txtstream.WriteLine("      </TablixRows>")
    txtstream.WriteLine("    </TablixBody>")
    txtstream.WriteLine("    <TablixColumnHierarchy>")
    txtstream.WriteLine("      <TablixMembers>")

For x As Integer = 0 To ns.Count - 1

    txtstream.WriteLine("        <TablixMember />")

Next

    txtstream.WriteLine("      </TablixMembers>")
    txtstream.WriteLine("    </TablixColumnHierarchy>")
    txtstream.WriteLine("    <TablixRowHierarchy>")
    txtstream.WriteLine("      <TablixMembers>")
    txtstream.WriteLine("        <TablixMember>")
    txtstream.WriteLine("          <KeepWithGroup>After</KeepWithGroup>")
    txtstream.WriteLine("        </TablixMember>")
    txtstream.WriteLine("        <TablixMember>")
    txtstream.WriteLine("          <Group Name=""Details"" />")
    txtstream.WriteLine("        </TablixMember>")
    txtstream.WriteLine("      </TablixMembers>")
    txtstream.WriteLine("    </TablixRowHierarchy>")
    txtstream.WriteLine("    <DataSetName>DataSet1</DataSetName>")
    txtstream.WriteLine("    <Height>0.5in</Height>")
    txtstream.WriteLine("    <Width>409.52083in</Width>")
    txtstream.WriteLine("    <Style>")
    txtstream.WriteLine("      <Border>")
    txtstream.WriteLine("        <Style>None</Style>")
    txtstream.WriteLine("      </Border>")
    txtstream.WriteLine("    </Style>")
    txtstream.WriteLine("  </Tablix>")
    txtstream.WriteLine("    </ReportItems>")
    txtstream.WriteLine("  <Height>2in</Height>")
    txtstream.WriteLine("  <Style />")
    txtstream.WriteLine(" </Body>")
    txtstream.WriteLine(" <Width>409.52083in</Width>")
    txtstream.WriteLine(" <Page>")
    txtstream.WriteLine("  <LeftMargin>1in</LeftMargin>")
    txtstream.WriteLine("  <RightMargin>1in</RightMargin>")
    txtstream.WriteLine("  <TopMargin>1in</TopMargin>")
    txtstream.WriteLine("  <BottomMargin>1in</BottomMargin>")
    txtstream.WriteLine("  <Style />")
    txtstream.WriteLine(" </Page>")
    txtstream.WriteLine(" <rd:ReportID>7fa7ad8c-6890-4152-8fce-3e6f01fffd8c</rd:ReportID>")
    txtstream.WriteLine(" <rd:ReportUnitType>Inch</rd:ReportUnitType>")
    txtstream.WriteLine("</Report>")
    txtstream.Close()
```

End Sub

Here's the code that generates the views for each ReportViewer:

```vb
Public Class Form1

    Public Structure Services
        Public Property AcceptPause As System.Boolean
        Public Property AcceptStop As System.Boolean
        Public Property Caption As System.String
        Public Property CheckPoint As System.Double
        Public Property CreationClassName As System.String
        Public Property Description As System.String
        Public Property DesktopInteract As System.Boolean
        Public Property DisplayName As System.String
        Public Property ErrorControl As System.String
        Public Property ExitCode As System.Double
        Public Property Name As System.String
        Public Property PathName As System.String
        Public Property ProcessId As System.Double
        Public Property ServiceSpecificExitCode As System.Double
        Public Property ServiceType As System.String
        Public Property Started As System.Boolean
        Public Property StartMode As System.String
        Public Property StartName As System.String
        Public Property State As System.String
        Public Property Status As System.String
        Public Property SystemCreationClassName As System.String
        Public Property SystemName As System.String
        Public Property TagId As System.Double
        Public Property WaitHint As System.Double
    End Structure


    Public Ds As DataSet
    Dim mcHammer As System.Collections.ObjectModel.Collection(Of Services) = New
System.Collections.ObjectModel.Collection(Of Services)
    Dim mcHammer1 As System.Collections.ObjectModel.Collection(Of Services) = New
System.Collections.ObjectModel.Collection(Of Services)
    Dim mcHammer2 As System.Collections.ObjectModel.Collection(Of Services) = New
System.Collections.ObjectModel.Collection(Of Services)

    Private Sub Form1_Load(ByVal sender As System.Object, ByVal e As System.EventArgs) Handles MyBase.Load


        Dim da As New OleDb.OleDbDataAdapter("Select * from [All Installed Services$]", _
"Provider=Microsoft.ACE.OLEDB.12.0;Extended Properties=""Excel 8.0;hdr=yes;Database=C:\Services.xlsx;"";")
        Dim dt As New DataTable
        da.Fill(dt)

        For Each row As DataRow In dt.Rows
            Dim myservices As New Services
            myservices.AcceptPause = row.Item("AcceptPause")
            myservices.AcceptStop = row.Item("AcceptStop")
            myservices.Caption = row.Item("Caption")
            myservices.CheckPoint = row.Item("CheckPoint")
            myservices.CreationClassName = row.Item("CreationClassName")
            myservices.Description = row.Item("Description")
            myservices.DesktopInteract = row.Item("DesktopInteract")
            myservices.DisplayName = row.Item("DisplayName")
            myservices.ErrorControl = row.Item("ErrorControl")
            myservices.ExitCode = row.Item("ExitCode")
```

```vbnet
            myservices.Name = row.Item("Name")
            myservices.PathName = row.Item("PathName")
            myservices.ProcessId = row.Item("ProcessId")
            myservices.ServiceSpecificExitCode = row.Item("ServiceSpecificExitCode")
            myservices.ServiceType = row.Item("ServiceType")
            myservices.Started = row.Item("Started")
            myservices.StartMode = row.Item("StartMode")
            myservices.StartName = row.Item("StartName")
            myservices.State = row.Item("State")
            myservices.Status = row.Item("Status")
            myservices.SystemCreationClassName = row.Item("SystemCreationClassName")
            myservices.SystemName = row.Item("SystemName")
            myservices.TagId = row.Item("TagId")
            myservices.WaitHint = row.Item("WaitHint")
            mcHammer.Add(myservices)
        Next

        ReportViewer1.LocalReport.ReportPath =
"C:\Users\Administrator\Desktop\Basic\WindowsApplication12\WindowsApplication12\AllInstalledServices.rdlc"
        ReportViewer1.LocalReport.DataSources.Clear()
        ReportViewer1.LocalReport.DataSources.Add(New
Microsoft.Reporting.WinForms.ReportDataSource("DataSet1", mcHammer))
        Me.ReportViewer1.RefreshReport()


        da = New OleDb.OleDbDataAdapter("Select * from [All Running Services$]",
"Provider=Microsoft.ACE.OLEDB.12.0;Extended Properties=""Excel 8.0;hdr=yes;Database=C:\Services.xlsx;"";")
        dt = New DataTable
        da.Fill(dt)

        For Each row As DataRow In dt.Rows
            Dim myservices As New Services
            myservices.AcceptPause = row.Item("AcceptPause")
            myservices.AcceptStop = row.Item("AcceptStop")
            myservices.Caption = row.Item("Caption")
            myservices.CheckPoint = row.Item("CheckPoint")
            myservices.CreationClassName = row.Item("CreationClassName")
            myservices.Description = row.Item("Description")
            myservices.DesktopInteract = row.Item("DesktopInteract")
            myservices.DisplayName = row.Item("DisplayName")
            myservices.ErrorControl = row.Item("ErrorControl")
            myservices.ExitCode = row.Item("ExitCode")
            myservices.Name = row.Item("Name")
            myservices.PathName = row.Item("PathName")
            myservices.ProcessId = row.Item("ProcessId")
            myservices.ServiceSpecificExitCode = row.Item("ServiceSpecificExitCode")
            myservices.ServiceType = row.Item("ServiceType")
            myservices.Started = row.Item("Started")
            myservices.StartMode = row.Item("StartMode")
            myservices.StartName = row.Item("StartName")
            myservices.State = row.Item("State")
            myservices.Status = row.Item("Status")
            myservices.SystemCreationClassName = row.Item("SystemCreationClassName")
            myservices.SystemName = row.Item("SystemName")
            myservices.TagId = row.Item("TagId")
            myservices.WaitHint = row.Item("WaitHint")
            mcHammer1.Add(myservices)
        Next

        ReportViewer2.LocalReport.ReportPath =
"C:\Users\Administrator\Desktop\Basic\WindowsApplication12\WindowsApplication12\AllRunningServices.rdlc"
        ReportViewer2.LocalReport.DataSources.Clear()
        ReportViewer2.LocalReport.DataSources.Add(New
Microsoft.Reporting.WinForms.ReportDataSource("DataSet1", mcHammer1))
        Me.ReportViewer2.RefreshReport()
```

```vbnet
    da = New OleDb.OleDbDataAdapter("Select * from [All Stopped Services$]",
"Provider=Microsoft.ACE.OLEDB.12.0;Extended Properties=""""Excel 8.0;hdr=yes;Database=C:\Services.xlsx;"""";")
    dt = New DataTable
    da.Fill(dt)

    For Each row As DataRow In dt.Rows
        Dim myservices As New Services
        myservices.AcceptPause = row.Item("AcceptPause")
        myservices.AcceptStop = row.Item("AcceptStop")
        myservices.Caption = row.Item("Caption")
        myservices.CheckPoint = row.Item("CheckPoint")
        myservices.CreationClassName = row.Item("CreationClassName")
        myservices.Description = row.Item("Description")
        myservices.DesktopInteract = row.Item("DesktopInteract")
        myservices.DisplayName = row.Item("DisplayName")
        myservices.ErrorControl = row.Item("ErrorControl")
        myservices.ExitCode = row.Item("ExitCode")
        myservices.Name = row.Item("Name")
        myservices.PathName = row.Item("PathName")
        myservices.ProcessId = row.Item("ProcessId")
        myservices.ServiceSpecificExitCode = row.Item("ServiceSpecificExitCode")
        myservices.ServiceType = row.Item("ServiceType")
        myservices.Started = row.Item("Started")
        myservices.StartMode = row.Item("StartMode")
        myservices.StartName = row.Item("StartName")
        myservices.State = row.Item("State")
        myservices.Status = row.Item("Status")
        myservices.SystemCreationClassName = row.Item("SystemCreationClassName")
        myservices.SystemName = row.Item("SystemName")
        myservices.TagId = row.Item("TagId")
        myservices.WaitHint = row.Item("WaitHint")
        mcHammer2.Add(myservices)
    Next

    ReportViewer3.LocalReport.ReportPath =
"C:\Users\Administrator\Desktop\Basic\WindowsApplication12\WindowsApplication12\AllStoppedServices.rdlc"
    ReportViewer3.LocalReport.DataSources.Clear()
    ReportViewer3.LocalReport.DataSources.Add(New
Microsoft.Reporting.WinForms.ReportDataSource("DataSet1", mcHammer2))
    Me.ReportViewer3.RefreshReport()

    End Sub
End Class
```

The results:

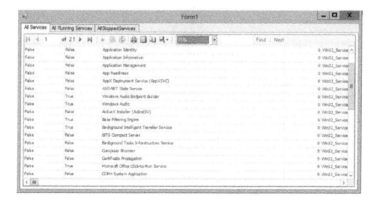

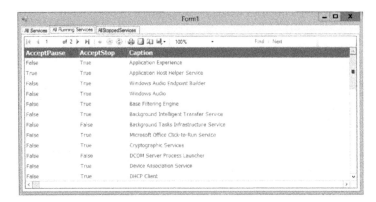

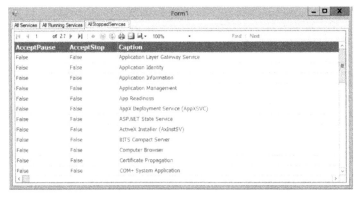

What is really going on here and why reports don't pay the bills

The chilling truth about reports

What is amazing – at least from my humble perspective – is the fact that many of the IT jobs programmers are being asked to do is have the ability to produce reports.

Well, programmers are programmers, testers are testers and report writers are report writers. Not everyone can be a programmer, a tester or a report writer.

Report writing is a very important skill set. An art. A visual form of communications. A necessary part in the completion of the information pipeline.

And yet, there are less people specializing in this profession then there are developers, engineers and program managers.

Not just write programs that accomplish tasks but do something with the information that suits the end users' need for a simple and to the point visualization of the data being produced by the program.

Almost every job I have worked over the past 20 years had the same problem. Tons of information but little to no way to display it.

There was a good reason for this lack of ability to take the results from the programming efforts and produce reports from it. Said simply, it isn't a programmer's job.

Programmers understand how a program should be written to produce results. That's where the imaginary line gets drawn in the sand and by all rights it should be.

After all, it takes a very dedicated kind of person to sit down in front of a computer and create on demand custom reports with the spit and polish needed to turn heads and hold the attention of CEOs and board members.

It is a different kind of energy needed to do that. Indeed, a very special kind of person. One that knows how to use Visual Studio and Blend. Who can add graphs and charts without hesitation? Who can put sexy into boring and come up with some amazing reports?

Honestly, I'm not one of them. But you might be. Which is why I've written this book. Not because I like to write reports but because I want to help you take the basics that are in this book, apply them to what you want to accomplish and, perhaps, put your creative talent to good use and produce truly amazing results.

Combining my basic and sometimes creative approach to producing reports is what I want to share with you – tribal knowledge, if you will – is where the two of us will share common ground.

I know reports from strictly a programmer's perspective and understand how they work. But you, on the other hand should easily be able to that and make a living from it.

Take the basics and do something with them that transcends what I know into something marvelous for your potential customers.

I lack the patience, or the finesse needed to turn the work into visually stunning reports. Perhaps that is your forte.

On the other hand, perhaps, it isn't.

Perhaps, you are being tasked by your employer to produce some reports before you end your latest contracting job and you are struggling, as I was, to wrap your head around these things known as reports.

One look at the internals of these things is enough to make you want to scream. At least, that was what I thought until I realized what was really going on under the hood.

Information used by both the RDLC and the RDL Files is not direct feed. What does that mean? It means you don't create a recordset and pump it directly into these reporting engines. We will talk more about that in the next chapter.

However, I am pointing this out here because I believe that half the reasons why these kinds of reports are seldom used by programmers is exactly for that reason.

Anyway, of all of the books I've done in the past couple of years, this one is the easiest to explain, easiest to write (because there is a lot of pictures and the code in it) and the work – if you call pressing a button work – can be 100% automated.

All of this is true! Problem is, I'm looking at 50 pages as I write this introduction and have realized I haven't said much. Which I can usually hear my imaginary choir singing "Hallelujah" so loudly that a plane 40,000 feet above my head would still think it is too loud.

Okay, so enough with my Edwards humor.

The purpose of this book is to get you to that point where the mechanics of creating reports no longer interferes with your ability to be as creative as you need to be and take the reports to the next level.

I don't pretend I am an expert at creating beautiful reports. In fact, if my job was solely dependent upon creating amazing looking reports I wouldn't last long.

But I am an expert problem solver. I can cut through the jungle of complexity and break things down in such a way that it makes sense and you can move forward in your understanding. I think I've already proved that resolving the issue with getting reports to work in Visual Studio 2019. That, to me and hopefully you will agree, would make programming reports much easier.

But what about really understanding what goes on behind the scenes? What is basic element XML? Can you use Attribute xml? What is an xsd file? How many different providers can be used with OleDb to produce these reports? How is it you can automate the process of creating the report file?

I'm about to answer all of these questions throughout the rest of this book.

The not always vital role the dataset plays in creating the xml and xsd files

It just doesn't do attribute xml

When it comes to using xml, xsd, the Report and the ReportViewer as a combination that works, the key to making the xml and the xsd is through the use of the dataset.

A couple of chapters back, I used the OleDbDataAdapter in combination with the DataTable. Let's take the same code and have it export both the xml and the xsd:

```
Dim da = New OleDb.OleDbDataAdapter("Select * from [All Running Services$]",
"Provider=Microsoft.ACE.OLEDB.12.0;Extended Properties=""Excel 8.0;hdr=yes;Database=C:\Services.xlsx;"";")
Dim dt = New DataTable
da.Fill(dt)
dt.TableName = "RunningServices"
dt.WriteXml(Application.StartupPath & "\RunningServices.xml")
dt.WriteXmlSchema(Application.StartupPath & "\RunningServices.xsd")
```

Below is one row from the xml:

```
<?xml version="1.0" standalone="yes"?>
<DocumentElement>
  <RunningServices>
    <AcceptPause>false</AcceptPause>
    <AcceptStop>true</AcceptStop>
    <Caption>Application Experience</Caption>
    <CheckPoint>0</CheckPoint>
    <CreationClassName>Win32_Service</CreationClassName>
    <Description>Processes application compatibility cache requests for applications as they are
launched</Description>
    <DesktopInteract>false</DesktopInteract>
    <DisplayName>Application Experience</DisplayName>
    <ErrorControl>Normal</ErrorControl>
    <ExitCode>0</ExitCode>
```

```
            <Name>Win32_Service</Name>
            <PathName>C:\\Windows\\system32\\svchost.exe -k netsvcs</PathName>
            <ProcessId>1028</ProcessId>
            <ServiceSpecificExitCode>0</ServiceSpecificExitCode>
            <ServiceType>Share Process</ServiceType>
            <Started>true</Started>
            <StartMode>Manual</StartMode>
            <StartName>localSystem</StartName>
            <State>Running</State>
            <Status>OK</Status>
          <SystemCreationClassName>Win32_ComputerSystem</SystemCreationClassName>
            <SystemName>WIN-VRKHLAOIDGT</SystemName>
            <TagId>0</TagId>
            <WaitHint>0</WaitHint>
          </RunningServices>
```

And the xsd:

```
<?xml version="1.0" standalone="yes"?>
<xs:schema        id="NewDataSet"        xmlns=""        xmlns:xs="http://www.w3.org/2001/XMLSchema"
xmlns:msdata="urn:schemas-microsoft-com:xml-msdata">
  <xs:element    name="NewDataSet"    msdata:IsDataSet="true"    msdata:MainDataTable="RunningServices"
msdata:UseCurrentLocale="true">
    <xs:complexType>
     <xs:choice minOccurs="0" maxOccurs="unbounded">
      <xs:element name="RunningServices">
       <xs:complexType>
        <xs:sequence>
         <xs:element name="AcceptPause" type="xs:boolean" minOccurs="0" />
         <xs:element name="AcceptStop" type="xs:boolean" minOccurs="0" />
         <xs:element name="Caption" type="xs:string" minOccurs="0" />
         <xs:element name="CheckPoint" type="xs:double" minOccurs="0" />
         <xs:element name="CreationClassName" type="xs:string" minOccurs="0" />
         <xs:element name="Description" type="xs:string" minOccurs="0" />
         <xs:element name="DesktopInteract" type="xs:boolean" minOccurs="0" />
         <xs:element name="DisplayName" type="xs:string" minOccurs="0" />
         <xs:element name="ErrorControl" type="xs:string" minOccurs="0" />
         <xs:element name="ExitCode" type="xs:double" minOccurs="0" />
         <xs:element name="InstallDate" type="xs:string" minOccurs="0" />
         <xs:element name="Name" type="xs:string" minOccurs="0" />
         <xs:element name="PathName" type="xs:string" minOccurs="0" />
         <xs:element name="ProcessId" type="xs:double" minOccurs="0" />
         <xs:element name="ServiceSpecificExitCode" type="xs:double" minOccurs="0" />
         <xs:element name="ServiceType" type="xs:string" minOccurs="0" />
         <xs:element name="Started" type="xs:boolean" minOccurs="0" />
         <xs:element name="StartMode" type="xs:string" minOccurs="0" />
         <xs:element name="StartName" type="xs:string" minOccurs="0" />
         <xs:element name="State" type="xs:string" minOccurs="0" />
         <xs:element name="Status" type="xs:string" minOccurs="0" />
         <xs:element name="SystemCreationClassName" type="xs:string" minOccurs="0" />
         <xs:element name="SystemName" type="xs:string" minOccurs="0" />
         <xs:element name="TagId" type="xs:double" minOccurs="0" />
         <xs:element name="WaitHint" type="xs:double" minOccurs="0" />
        </xs:sequence>
       </xs:complexType>
      </xs:element>
     </xs:choice>
    </xs:complexType>
  </xs:element>
</xs:schema>
```

Now, compare the xsd to the structure I used previously:

```
Public Structure Services
    Public Property AcceptPause As System.Boolean
```

```
      Public Property AcceptStop As System.Boolean
      Public Property Caption As System.String
      Public Property CheckPoint As System.Double
      Public Property CreationClassName As System.String
      Public Property Description As System.String
      Public Property DesktopInteract As System.Boolean
      Public Property DisplayName As System.String
      Public Property ErrorControl As System.String
      Public Property ExitCode As System.Double
      Public Property Name As System.String
      Public Property PathName As System.String
      Public Property ProcessId As System.Double
      Public Property ServiceSpecificExitCode As System.Double
      Public Property ServiceType As System.String
      Public Property Started As System.Boolean
      Public Property StartMode As System.String
      Public Property StartName As System.String
      Public Property State As System.String
      Public Property Status As System.String
      Public Property SystemCreationClassName As System.String
      Public Property SystemName As System.String
      Public Property TagId As System.Double
      Public Property WaitHint As System.Double
   End Structure
```

A structure looks very similar to the xsd (XML Schema Definition) – without, of course, all the xml. They define what will be accepted as the fields (or columns, properties) that will be used coupled with the data types.

```
   Public Class Products

      Private Property mnuAcceptPause As System.Boolean
      Private Property mnuAcceptStop As System.Boolean
      Private Property mnuCaption As System.String
      Private Property mnuCheckPoint As System.Double
      Private Property mnuCreationClassName As System.String
      Private Property mnuDescription As System.String
      Private Property mnuDesktopInteract As System.Boolean
      Private Property mnuDisplayName As System.String
      Private Property mnuErrorControl As System.String
      Private Property mnuExitCode As System.Double
      Private Property mnuName As System.String
      Private Property mnuPathName As System.String
      Private Property mnuProcessId As System.Double
      Private Property mnuServiceSpecificExitCode As System.Double
      Private Property mnuServiceType As System.String
      Private Property mnuStarted As System.Boolean
      Private Property mnuStartMode As System.String
      Private Property mnuStartName As System.String
      Private Property mnuState As System.String
      Private Property mnuStatus As System.String
      Private Property mnuSystemCreationClassName As System.String
      Private Property mnuSystemName As System.String
      Private Property mnuTagId As System.Double
      Private Property mnuWaitHint As System.Double



      Public Property AcceptPause() As System.Boolean
         Get
            AcceptPause = mnuAcceptPause
         End Get
         Set(ByVal value As System.Boolean)
```

```vbnet
                mnuAcceptPause = value
            End Set
        End Property
        Public Property AcceptStop As System.Boolean

            Get
                AcceptStop = mnuAcceptStop
            End Get
            Set(ByVal value As System.Boolean)
                mnuAcceptStop = value
            End Set

        End Property

        Public Property Caption As System.String
            Get
                Caption = mnuCaption
            End Get
            Set(ByVal value As System.String)
                mnuCaption = value
            End Set
        End Property
        Public Property CheckPoint As System.Double
            Get
                CheckPoint = mnuCheckPoint
            End Get
            Set(ByVal value As System.Double)
                mnuCheckPoint = value
            End Set
        End Property
        Public Property CreationClassName As System.String
            Get
                CreationClassName = mnuCreationClassName
            End Get
            Set(ByVal value As System.String)
                mnuCreationClassName = value
            End Set
        End Property
        Public Property Description As System.String
            Get
                Description = mnuDescription
            End Get
            Set(ByVal value As System.String)
                mnuDescription = value
            End Set
        End Property
        Public Property DesktopInteract As System.Boolean
            Get
                DesktopInteract = mnuDesktopInteract
            End Get
            Set(ByVal value As System.Boolean)
                mnuDesktopInteract = value
            End Set
        End Property
        Public Property DisplayName As System.String
            Get
                DisplayName = mnuDisplayName
            End Get
            Set(ByVal value As System.String)
                mnuDisplayName = value
            End Set
        End Property
        Public Property ErrorControl As System.String
            Get
                ErrorControl = mnuErrorControl
            End Get
```

```vb
      Set(ByVal value As System.String)
         mnuErrorControl = value
      End Set
   End Property
   Public Property ExitCode As System.Double
      Get
         ExitCode = mnuExitCode
      End Get
      Set(ByVal value As System.Double)
         mnuExitCode = value
      End Set
   End Property
   Public Property Name As System.String
      Get
         Name = mnuName
      End Get
      Set(ByVal value As System.String)
         mnuName = value
      End Set
   End Property
   Public Property PathName As System.String
      Get
         PathName = mnuPathName
      End Get
      Set(ByVal value As System.String)
         mnuPathName = value
      End Set
   End Property
   Public Property ProcessId As System.Double
      Get
         ProcessId = mnuProcessId
      End Get
      Set(ByVal value As System.Double)
         mnuProcessId = value
      End Set
   End Property
   Public Property ServiceSpecificExitCode As System.Double
      Get
         ServiceSpecificExitCode = mnuServiceSpecificExitCode
      End Get
      Set(ByVal value As System.Double)
         mnuServiceSpecificExitCode = value
      End Set
   End Property
   Public Property ServiceType As System.String
      Get
         ServiceType = mnuServiceType
      End Get
      Set(ByVal value As System.String)
         mnuServiceType = value
      End Set
   End Property
   Public Property Started As System.Boolean
      Get
         Started = mnuStarted
      End Get
      Set(ByVal value As System.Boolean)
         mnuStarted = value
      End Set
   End Property
   Public Property StartMode As System.String
      Get
         StartMode = mnuStartMode
      End Get
      Set(ByVal value As System.String)
         mnuStartMode = value
```

```vbnet
      End Set
   End Property
   Public Property StartName As System.String
      Get
         StartName = mnuStartName
      End Get
      Set(ByVal value As System.String)
         mnuStartName = value
      End Set
   End Property
   Public Property State As System.String
      Get
         State = mnuState
      End Get
      Set(ByVal value As System.String)
         mnuState = value
      End Set
   End Property
   Public Property Status As System.String
      Get
         Status = mnuStatus
      End Get
      Set(ByVal value As System.String)
         mnuStatus = value
      End Set
   End Property
   Public Property SystemCreationClassName As System.String
      Get
         SystemCreationClassName = mnuSystemCreationClassName
      End Get
      Set(ByVal value As System.String)
         mnuSystemCreationClassName = value
      End Set
   End Property
   Public Property SystemName As System.String
      Get
         SystemName = mnuSystemName
      End Get
      Set(ByVal value As System.String)
         mnuSystemName = value
      End Set
   End Property
   Public Property TagId As System.Double
      Get
         TagId = mnuTagId
      End Get
      Set(ByVal value As System.Double)
         mnuTagId = value
      End Set
   End Property
   Public Property WaitHint As System.Double
      Get
         WaitHint = mnuWaitHint
      End Get
      Set(ByVal value As System.Double)
         mnuWaitHint = value
      End Set
   End Property

End Class
```

Do we really need it?

No.

Why?

Because this code uses an IEnumerable object:

```
ReportViewer1.LocalReport.DataSources.Clear()
ReportViewer1.LocalReport.DataSources.Add(New
Microsoft.Reporting.WinForms.ReportDataSource("DataSet1", mcHammer))
Me.ReportViewer1.RefreshReport()
```

Which means you could also use a DataSet, a DataTable or a DataView. The DataSet would replace mcHammer with:

Dim ds as new DataSet	ds.Tables(0)
Dim dt as new DataTable	dt
Using one of the above	ds.Tables(0).DefaultView or dt.DefaultView

No xsd, structure or class is needed. Below is the code:

```
ReportViewer3.LocalReport.ReportPath =
"C:\Users\Administrator\Desktop\Basic\WindowsApplication12\WindowsApplication12\AllStoppedServices.rdlc"
ReportViewer3.LocalReport.DataSources.Clear()
ReportViewer3.LocalReport.DataSources.Add(New
Microsoft.Reporting.WinForms.ReportDataSource("DataSet1", ds.Tables(0)))
Me.ReportViewer3.RefreshReport()
```

Here's the view:

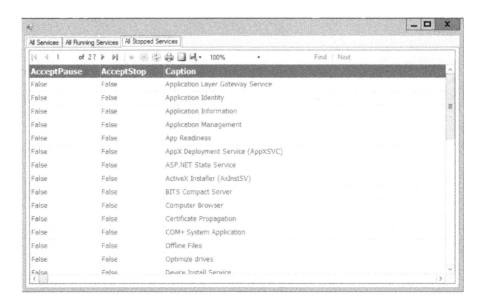

So why use then in the first place?

If you only wanted to use OleDb, then I suppose it would be a complete and total waste of time and 1 second button clicks to create the class or structure needed to dynamically populate the Report. And let's face it, all three ways to populate the report dynamically work without issue.

Where the structure, class or xsd serve to support what we want to get accomplished is when we want to create reports that have no direct database collections of columns and rows. Things like creating reports from registry entries, event logs and WMI Classes.

Now I can hear the argument already: "But you just used Win32_Services to create a report didn't you?"

Yes, I did. But for more than one reason. First, I showed you how to connect to an Excel spreadsheet using an ISAM, I also showed you how you can use a spreadsheet to create a report, I showed you how you can dynamically build all of this through code and polish it off using OleDb.

That's a lot off good work and example code.

Putting the Report.rdlc file
under the microscope
It looks harder to work with then it really is

If you have never opened a rdlc file in notepad, please do so. I was going to do it here, but it is taking up too many pages. Here, I just want to show you the code and explain what each section is doing:

I need two arrays that will be used to get a list of names and widths for each entry (or column):

Public ns() As String
Public l() As Integer

Public Sub Create_THE_RDLC_FILE(ByVal RName As String)

I create a FileSystemObject to create the file:

Dim fso As Object = CreateObject("Scripting.FileSystemObject")
Dim txtstream As Object = fso.OpenTextFile(Application.StartupPath & "\" & RName & ".rdlc", 2, True, -2)

I then coped a pasted a standard RDLC file into the routine, added addition quotes where needed and added the txtstream.WriteLine to each line:

```
txtstream.WriteLine("<?xml version=""1.0""?>")
txtstream.WriteLine("<Report
xmlns:rd=""http://schemas.microsoft.com/SQLServer/reporting/reportdesigner""
xmlns=""http://schemas.microsoft.com/sqlserver/reporting/2008/01/reportdefinitio
n"">")
txtstream.WriteLine("  <DataSources>")
txtstream.WriteLine("    <DataSource Name=""WindowsApplication5"">")
txtstream.WriteLine("      <ConnectionProperties>")
txtstream.WriteLine("
<DataProvider>System.Data.DataSet</DataProvider>")
txtstream.WriteLine("        <ConnectString>/* Local Connection
*/</ConnectString>")
txtstream.WriteLine("      </ConnectionProperties>")
txtstream.WriteLine("      <rd:DataSourceID>4ada475a-519d-4774-8a8e-
cd804357bc15</rd:DataSourceID>")
txtstream.WriteLine("    </DataSource>")
txtstream.WriteLine("  </DataSources>")
txtstream.WriteLine("  <DataSets>")
txtstream.WriteLine("    <DataSet Name=""DataSet1"">")
txtstream.WriteLine("      <Fields>")
```

I removed all the existing fields except one and used that to add a field name for each name in my collection of names:

```
For x As Integer = 0 To ns.Count - 1

    txtstream.WriteLine("        <Field Name=""" & ns(x) & """>")
    txtstream.WriteLine("          <DataField>" & ns(x) & "</DataField>")
    txtstream.WriteLine("
<rd:TypeName>System.String</rd:TypeName>")
    txtstream.WriteLine("        </Field>")
```

Next

I left this as is because the code in the man form clears all the DataSources anyway:

```
        txtstream.WriteLine("    </Fields>")
        txtstream.WriteLine("    <Query>")
        txtstream.WriteLine("
<DataSourceName>WindowsApplication5</DataSourceName>")
        txtstream.WriteLine("                    <CommandText>/* Local Query
*/</CommandText>")
        txtstream.WriteLine("    </Query>")
        txtstream.WriteLine("    <rd:DataSetInfo>")
        txtstream.WriteLine("
<rd:DataSetName>WindowsApplication5</rd:DataSetName>")
        txtstream.WriteLine("      <rd:TableName>data</rd:TableName>")
        txtstream.WriteLine("
<rd:ObjectDataSourceSelectMethod>win32_bios</rd:ObjectDataSourceSelectMethod
>")
        txtstream.WriteLine("
<rd:ObjectDataSourceType>WindowsApplication5.data,      win32_bios.Designer.vb,
Version=0.0.0.0,                              Culture=neutral,
PublicKeyToken=null</rd:ObjectDataSourceType>")
        txtstream.WriteLine("    </rd:DataSetInfo>")
        txtstream.WriteLine("  </DataSet>")
        txtstream.WriteLine("  </DataSets>")
        txtstream.WriteLine("  <Body>")
        txtstream.WriteLine("    <ReportItems>")
        txtstream.WriteLine("      <Tablix Name=""Tablix1"">")
        txtstream.WriteLine("        <TablixBody>")
        txtstream.WriteLine("          <TablixColumns>")
```

This is where you can save a lot of time and effort by auto adjusting the width of each column to avoid having to manually adjust the width of each column by hand. My measurements were based on the Spreadsheet's Column width:

```
For x As Integer = 0 To ns.GetLength(0) - 1
    l(x) = ws1.Columns(x + 1).Width
Next
```

I still had to do some fine tuning to get the width to render each name and value without bleeding into an additional new line:

```
For x As Integer = 0 To ns.Count - 1

    txtstream.WriteLine("          <TablixColumn>")
    txtstream.WriteLine("          <Width>" & l(x) / 46 & "in</Width>")
    txtstream.WriteLine("          </TablixColumn>")

Next

txtstream.WriteLine("     </TablixColumns>")
txtstream.WriteLine("     <TablixRows>")
txtstream.WriteLine("      <TablixRow>")
txtstream.WriteLine("       <Height>0.25in</Height>")
txtstream.WriteLine("       <TablixCells>")
```

This next routine added the caption textboxes to the report:

```
For x As Integer = 0 To ns.Count - 1
```

```vb
            txtstream.WriteLine("          <TablixCell>")
            txtstream.WriteLine("           <CellContents>")
            txtstream.WriteLine("            <Textbox Name=""""Textbox"" & x + 1 &
"""">")
            txtstream.WriteLine("             <CanGrow>true</CanGrow>")
            txtstream.WriteLine("
<KeepTogether>true</KeepTogether>")
            txtstream.WriteLine("             <Paragraphs>")
            txtstream.WriteLine("              <Paragraph>")
            txtstream.WriteLine("               <TextRuns>")
            txtstream.WriteLine("                <TextRun>")
            txtstream.WriteLine("                 <Value>" & ns(x) & "</Value>")
            txtstream.WriteLine("                 <Style>")
            txtstream.WriteLine("
<FontFamily>Tahoma</FontFamily>")
            txtstream.WriteLine("                  <FontSize>11pt</FontSize>")
            txtstream.WriteLine("
<FontWeight>Bold</FontWeight>")
            txtstream.WriteLine("                  <Color>White</Color>")
            txtstream.WriteLine("                 </Style>")
            txtstream.WriteLine("                </TextRun>")
            txtstream.WriteLine("               </TextRuns>")
            txtstream.WriteLine("               <Style />")
            txtstream.WriteLine("              </Paragraph>")
            txtstream.WriteLine("             </Paragraphs>")
            txtstream.WriteLine("             <rd:DefaultName>Textbox" & x + 1 &
"</rd:DefaultName>")
            txtstream.WriteLine("             <Style>")
            txtstream.WriteLine("              <Border>")
            txtstream.WriteLine("               <Color>#7292cc</Color>")
            txtstream.WriteLine("               <Style>Solid</Style>")
            txtstream.WriteLine("              </Border>")
```

```vbnet
        txtstream.WriteLine("
<BackgroundColor>#4c68a2</BackgroundColor>")
            txtstream.WriteLine("                    <PaddingLeft>2pt</PaddingLeft>")
            txtstream.WriteLine("
<PaddingRight>2pt</PaddingRight>")
            txtstream.WriteLine("                    <PaddingTop>2pt</PaddingTop>")
            txtstream.WriteLine("
<PaddingBottom>2pt</PaddingBottom>")
            txtstream.WriteLine("                    </Style>")
            txtstream.WriteLine("                </Textbox>")
            txtstream.WriteLine("            </CellContents>")
            txtstream.WriteLine("            </TablixCell>")

    Next


        txtstream.WriteLine("        </TablixCells>")
        txtstream.WriteLine("        </TablixRow>")
        txtstream.WriteLine("        <TablixRow>")
        txtstream.WriteLine("            <Height>0.25in</Height>")
        txtstream.WriteLine("            <TablixCells>")
```

This routine adds the value textboxes to the report:

```vbnet
    For x As Integer = 0 To ns.Count - 1

        txtstream.WriteLine("            <TablixCell>")
        txtstream.WriteLine("            <CellContents>")
        txtstream.WriteLine("                <Textbox Name=""" & ns(x) & """>")
        txtstream.WriteLine("                    <CanGrow>true</CanGrow>")
        txtstream.WriteLine("
<KeepTogether>true</KeepTogether>")
        txtstream.WriteLine("                    <Paragraphs>")
```

```
txtstream.WriteLine("              <Paragraph>")
txtstream.WriteLine("                <TextRuns>")
txtstream.WriteLine("                  <TextRun>")
txtstream.WriteLine("                    <Value>=Fields!" & ns(x) &
".Value</Value>")
txtstream.WriteLine("                    <Style>")
txtstream.WriteLine("
<FontFamily>Tahoma</FontFamily>")
txtstream.WriteLine("                      <Color>#4d4d4d</Color>")
txtstream.WriteLine("                    </Style>")
txtstream.WriteLine("                  </TextRun>")
txtstream.WriteLine("                </TextRuns>")
txtstream.WriteLine("                <Style />")
txtstream.WriteLine("              </Paragraph>")
txtstream.WriteLine("            </Paragraphs>")
txtstream.WriteLine("                <rd:DefaultName>" & ns(x) &
"</rd:DefaultName>")
txtstream.WriteLine("            <Style>")
txtstream.WriteLine("              <Border>")
txtstream.WriteLine("                <Color>#e5e5e5</Color>")
txtstream.WriteLine("                <Style>Solid</Style>")
txtstream.WriteLine("              </Border>")
txtstream.WriteLine("              <PaddingLeft>2pt</PaddingLeft>")
txtstream.WriteLine("
<PaddingRight>2pt</PaddingRight>")
txtstream.WriteLine("              <PaddingTop>2pt</PaddingTop>")
txtstream.WriteLine("
<PaddingBottom>2pt</PaddingBottom>")
txtstream.WriteLine("            </Style>")
txtstream.WriteLine("          </Textbox>")
txtstream.WriteLine("        </CellContents>")
txtstream.WriteLine("      </TablixCell>")
```

```vb
Next

        txtstream.WriteLine("            </TablixCells>")
        txtstream.WriteLine("          </TablixRow>")
        txtstream.WriteLine("        </TablixRows>")
        txtstream.WriteLine("      </TablixBody>")
        txtstream.WriteLine("      <TablixColumnHierarchy>")
        txtstream.WriteLine("        <TablixMembers>")
```

This next routine adds a placeholder for each field:

```vb
For x As Integer = 0 To ns.Count - 1
    txtstream.WriteLine("          <TablixMember />")
Next

        txtstream.WriteLine("        </TablixMembers>")
        txtstream.WriteLine("      </TablixColumnHierarchy>")
        txtstream.WriteLine("      <TablixRowHierarchy>")
        txtstream.WriteLine("        <TablixMembers>")
        txtstream.WriteLine("          <TablixMember>")
        txtstream.WriteLine("
<KeepWithGroup>After</KeepWithGroup>")
        txtstream.WriteLine("          </TablixMember>")
        txtstream.WriteLine("          <TablixMember>")
        txtstream.WriteLine("            <Group Name=""Details"" />")
        txtstream.WriteLine("          </TablixMember>")
        txtstream.WriteLine("        </TablixMembers>")
        txtstream.WriteLine("      </TablixRowHierarchy>")
        txtstream.WriteLine("      <DataSetName>DataSet1</DataSetName>")
        txtstream.WriteLine("      <Height>0.5in</Height>")
        txtstream.WriteLine("      <Width>409.52083in</Width>")
        txtstream.WriteLine("      <Style>")
        txtstream.WriteLine("        <Border>")
```

```
txtstream.WriteLine("        <Style>None</Style>")
txtstream.WriteLine("       </Border>")
txtstream.WriteLine("      </Style>")
txtstream.WriteLine("     </Tablix>")
txtstream.WriteLine("   </ReportItems>")
txtstream.WriteLine("   <Height>2in</Height>")
txtstream.WriteLine("   <Style />")
txtstream.WriteLine("  </Body>")
txtstream.WriteLine("  <Width>409.52083in</Width>")
txtstream.WriteLine("  <Page>")
txtstream.WriteLine("    <LeftMargin>1in</LeftMargin>")
txtstream.WriteLine("    <RightMargin>1in</RightMargin>")
txtstream.WriteLine("    <TopMargin>1in</TopMargin>")
txtstream.WriteLine("    <BottomMargin>1in</BottomMargin>")
txtstream.WriteLine("    <Style />")
txtstream.WriteLine("  </Page>")
txtstream.WriteLine("  <rd:ReportID>7fa7ad8c-6890-4152-8fce-3e6f01fffd8c</rd:ReportID>")
txtstream.WriteLine("  <rd:ReportUnitType>Inch</rd:ReportUnitType>")
txtstream.WriteLine("</Report>")
txtstream.Close()

    End Sub
```

And we are done automating the report. It is just that simple.

Some questions you may want answered

Question: I have an older version of a report program, can I use it in Visual Studio 2019 Community Edition?

Yes. But remember one thing, the drop down you normally expect to use to set the location of the report location and other properties the drop down would provide you will not work .

Apparently, the control thinks it is in run mode and not design mode.

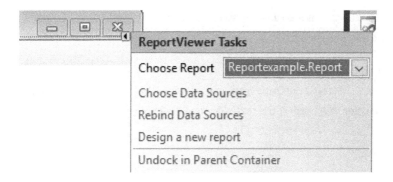

| ◄ ◄ 1 | of 2? ► ►| | ⊕ ⊗ ⊕ | ⎙ ☐ ⎘ ◄▪ ▾ | 100% | ▾ | Find : Next | | |

Product ID	Product Name	Supplier ID	Category ID	Quantity Per Unit	Unit Price	Units
1	Chai	1	1	10 boxes x 20 bags	18	39
2	Chang	1	1	24 - 12 oz bottles	19	17
3	Aniseed Syrup	1	2	12 - 550 ml bottles	10	13
4	Chef Anton's Cajun Seasoning	2	2	48 - 6 oz jars	22	53
5	Chef Anton's Gumbo Mix	2	2	36 boxes	21.35	0
6	Grandma's Boysenberry Spread	3	2	12 - 8 oz jars	25	120
7	Uncle Bob's Organic Dried Pears	3	7	12 - 1 lb pkgs	30	15
8	Northwoods Cranberry Sauce	3	2	12 - 12 oz jars	40	6
9	Mishi Kobe Niku	4	6	18 - 500 g pkgs	97	29
10	Ikura	4	8	12 - 200 ml jars	31	31
11	Queso Cabrales	5	4	1 kg pkg	21	22
12	Queso Manchego La Pastora	5	4	10 - 500 g pkgs	38	86
13	Konbu	6	8	2 kg box	6	24
14	Tofu	6	7	40 - 100 g pkgs	23.25	35
15	Genen Shouyu	6	2	24 - 250 ml bottles	15.5	39
16	Pavlova	7	3	32 - 500 g boxes	17.45	29

Otherwise, as shown above, importing the solution into VB.Net works perfectly fine. Which raises the next question.

Question: Can I add the control at runtime?

Answer: Yes, here's the code:

```
Dim ReportViewer1 As New Microsoft.Reporting.WinForms.ReportViewer
Me.Controls.Add(ReportViewer1)
ReportViewer1.Dock = DockStyle.Fill
```

Question: Can I change the font?

Answer: Yes.   In fact, not only can you change the font, you can change the background color, the border, the text color and a whole lot more.

Here's an example of playing around with the properties:

Form1

Product ID	Product Name	Supplier ID	Category ID	Quantity Per Unit	Unit Price	Units In Stock	U
1	Chai	1	1	10 boxes x 20 bags	18	39	0
2	Chang	1	1	24 - 12 oz bottles	19	17	4
3	Aniseed Syrup	1	2	12 - 550 ml bottles	10	13	7
4	Chef Anton's Cajun Seasoning	2	2	48 - 6 oz jars	22	53	0
5	Chef Anton's Gumbo Mix	2	2	36 boxes	21.35	0	0
6	Grandma's Boysenberry Spread	3	2	12 - 8 oz jars	25	120	0
7	Uncle Bob's Organic Dried Pears	3	7	12 - 1 lb pkgs.	30	15	0
8	Northwoods Cranberry Sauce	3	2	12 - 12 oz jars	40	6	0
9	Mishi Kobe Niku	4	6	18 - 500 g pkgs.	97	29	0
10	Ikura	4	8	12 - 200 ml jars	31	31	0
11	Queso Cabrales	5	4	1 kg pkg.	21	22	3
12	Queso Manchego La Pastora	5	4	10 - 500 g pkgs.	38	86	0
13	Konbu	6	8	2 kg box	6	24	0
14	Tofu	6	7	40 - 100 g pkgs.	23.25	35	0
15	Genen Shouyu	6	2	24 - 250 ml	15.5	39	0

Question: Can I replace the DataSource with OLEDB Code?

Answer: Yes, you can. As long as the columns are the same as the ones listed in the xsd file that you are using, you can dynamically use the DataSet, DataTable or the DataView to populate the report. Below is a table that shows what you need to make it work.

Dim ds as new DataSet	ds.Tables(0)
Dim dt as new DataTable	dt
Using one of the above	ds.Tables(0).DefaultView or dt.DefaultView

Question: I want to manually add or change the Report to include changes I made to Field names using the xml editor. But when I do, I either get a blank report or the changes aren't seen. What's wrong?

Answer: Well there could be two things going on which you need to know about.

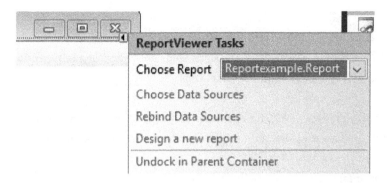

Question: Should I use the Wizard or create the report manually?

Answer: Either choice goes through the same steps once you add a table to the report. So, either way, you go through the same steps:

So, what is going on here? Well, for one thing, it should be obvious that this xsd file is describing the layout of the xml and, most importantly, the way in which it should be rendered.

As a matter of fact, that link above in the xsd file provides you with a whole lot of more misery trying to figure out what the heck this type of file is and how that file produces additional files inside the IDE.

XML Schema

15 October 2014

Table of contents

Introduction

This document describes the XML Schema namespace. It also contains a directory of links to these related resources, using Resource Directory Description Language.

Related Resources for XML Schema

Schemas for XML Schema

DTD

XML Schema 1.1

A (non-normative) DTD XMLSchema.dtd for XML Schema. It incorporates an auxiliary DTD, datatypes.dtd.

XML Schema 1.0

A (non-normative) DTD XMLSchema.dtd for XML Schema. It incorporates an auxiliary DTD, datatypes.dtd.

XML Schema

XML Schema 1.1

An XML Schema schema document for XML Schema schema documents.

XML Schema 1.0

An XML Schema schema document for XML Schema schema documents. Last updated with release of XML Schema 2nd edition in July 2004.

Normative References

1. W3C XML Schema Definition Language (XSD) 1.1 Part 1: Structures, W3C XML Schema Definition Language (XSD) 1.1 Part 2: Datatypes
2. XML Schema Part 1: Structures (2nd Edition), XML Schema Part 2: Datatypes (2nd Edition), XML Schema Part 0: Primer (2nd Edition)
3. XPath and XQuery Functions and Operators 3.1 introduces a new type, xs:numeric, that is a union of xs:decimal, xs:float, and xs:double.

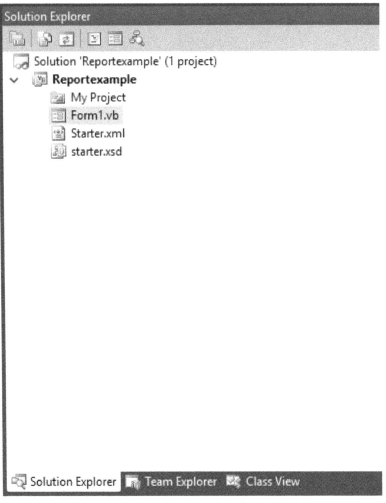

As you can see, there is nothing here but the xml (which, since the xsd helped to add some additional stuff, I've added to the xml).

Now, what I want to do is create a report.

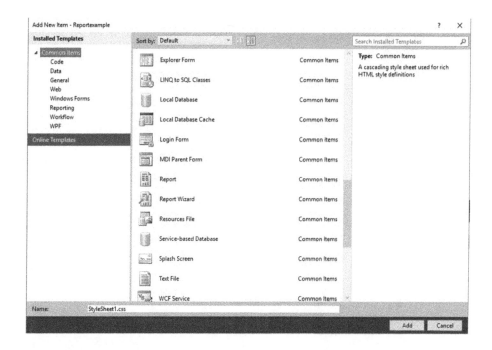

I have two choices. I can use the wizard, or I can manually do the same thing selecting a report. I've decided to use the report wizard first. So, I click on that.

The first thing the report wizard wants to do is create a dataset. But to do this, it needs to know where and what the name of the Data Source is.

So, I click on new and it gives me the option to select what type of data source I want to use.

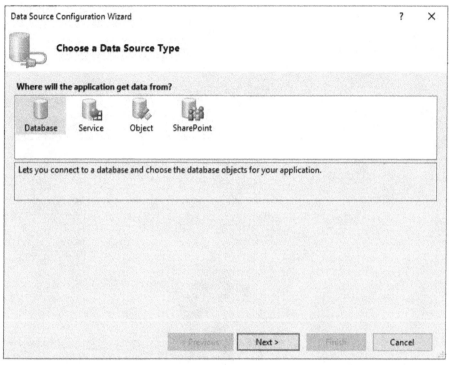

Since I'm not using a Database, Service or SharePoint, I highlight Object and click next.

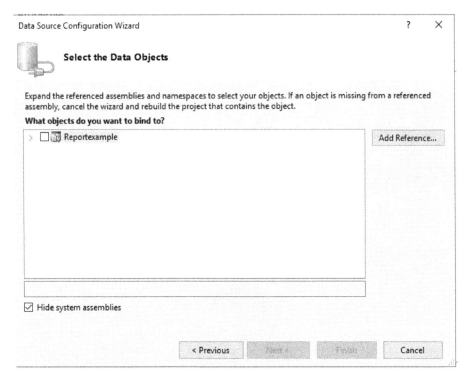

I am now back into my solution explorer.

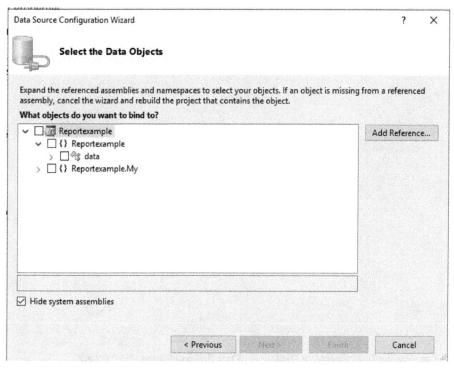

After expanding a few nodes, it doesn't take too many clicks to see a familiar name. So, I check data and click finish.

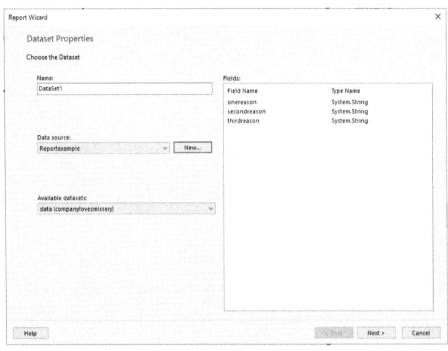

I now have a Data Source, a Dataset and my three columns. I click next.

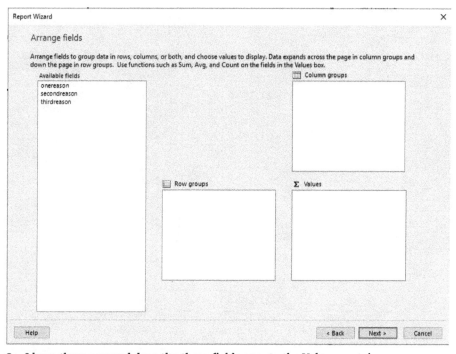

So, I have three raw and drop the three fields over to the Values container.

Once done, I click next, next and next. I then stretch the table out to fill the report area.

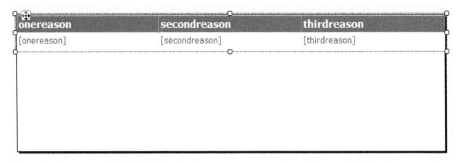

Now, I want to add a Report Viewer control to my form.

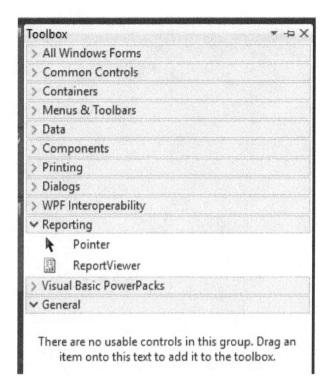

I then dock the control and add my report where it says Choose Report as shown below.

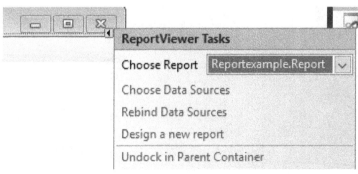

I then run the application.

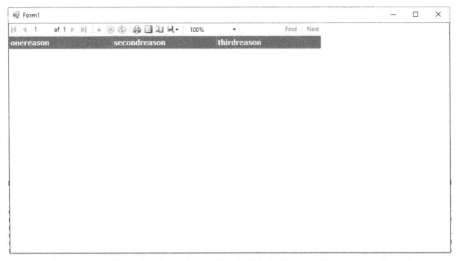

Oops! Forgot to bind the data. (Actually, I didn't forget. I just wanted to show you what happens of you do.)

So, I'm going to get the full file path by clicking the xml file and looking for it in the properties:

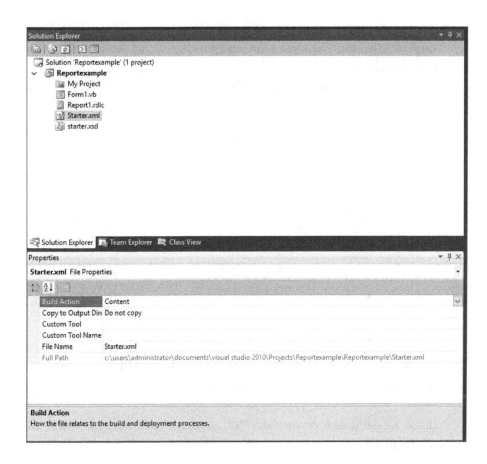

```vb
Dim ds As New System.Data.DataSet
ds.ReadXml("c:\users\administrator\documents\visual studio
2010\Projects\Reportexample\Reportexample\Starter.xml")
dataBindingSource.DataSource = ds
Me.ReportViewer1.RefreshR
```

Question: You mentioned that I can use both element and attribute xml, what should each look like?

Answer: Here's what the Element XML looks like:

```xml
<?xml version="1.0" encoding="utf-8"?>
<data>
  <companylovesmissery>
    <onereason>onereason1</onereason>
    <secondreason>secondreason1</secondreason>
    <thirdreason>thirdreason1</thirdreason>
  </companylovesmissery>
  <companylovesmissery>
    <onereason>onereason2</onereason>
    <secondreason>secondreason2</secondreason>
    <thirdreason>thirdreason2</thirdreason>
  </companylovesmissery>
  <companylovesmissery>
    <onereason>onereason3</onereason>
    <secondreason>secondreason3</secondreason>
    <thirdreason>thirdreason3</thirdreason>
  </companylovesmissery>
</data>
```

Notice that there is a processing instruction, a root node, a list of nodes (nodelist) which are the same thing as a row collection and within that collection another collection of columns. Clean, simple and to the point.

All you are doing with the Attribute XML creating a node name and adding the column collection elements to the same line:

```xml
<?xml version="1.0" encoding="utf-8"?>
<data>
  <companylovesmissery>
    <properties onereason="onereason1"  secondreason="secondreason1"  thirdreason = "thirdreason1"/>
  </companylovesmissery>
  <companylovesmissery>
    <properties onereason="onereason2"  secondreason="secondreason2"  thirdreason = "thirdreason2"/>
  </companylovesmissery>
  <companylovesmissery>
    <properties onereason="onereason3"  secondreason="secondreason3"  thirdreason = "thirdreason3"/>
  </companylovesmissery>
</data>
```

Now, let's take this and turn it into xsd and do the same with the element xml and see it there's anything to concern ourselves with.

Here is the Attribute xsd:

```xml
<?xml version="1.0" standalone="yes"?>
<xs:schema id="data" xmlns="" xmlns:xs="http://www.w3.org/2001/XMLSchema"
xmlns:msdata="urn:schemas-microsoft-com:xml-msdata">
    <xs:element name="data" msdata:IsDataSet="true" msdata:UseCurrentLocale="true">
     <xs:complexType>
      <xs:choice minOccurs="0" maxOccurs="unbounded">
       <xs:element name="companylovesmissery">
        <xs:complexType>
         <xs:attribute name="reason1" type="xs:string" />
         <xs:attribute name="reason2" type="xs:string" />
         <xs:attribute name="reason3" type="xs:string" />
        </xs:complexType>
       </xs:element>
      </xs:choice>
     </xs:complexType>
    </xs:element>
   </xs:schema>
```

Here is the element xsd:

```xml
<?xml version="1.0" standalone="yes"?>
<xs:schema id="data" xmlns="" xmlns:xs="http://www.w3.org/2001/XMLSchema"
xmlns:msdata="urn:schemas-microsoft-com:xml-msdata">
 <xs:element name="data" msdata:IsDataSet="true" msdata:UseCurrentLocale="true">
  <xs:complexType>
   <xs:choice minOccurs="0" maxOccurs="unbounded">
    <xs:element name="companylovesmissery">
     <xs:complexType>
      <xs:sequence>
       <xs:element name="onereason" type="xs:string" minOccurs="0" />
       <xs:element name="secondreason" type="xs:string" minOccurs="0" />
       <xs:element name="thirdreason" type="xs:string" minOccurs="0" />
      </xs:sequence>
     </xs:complexType>
    </xs:element>
   </xs:choice>
  </xs:complexType>
 </xs:element>
</xs:schema>
```

Do you see the difference? In the Element XML, the tag: <xs:sequence> has bee added to mark the elements as having on or more than one numerations of each element. Here's the Attribute XML version running in Visual Studio 2019:

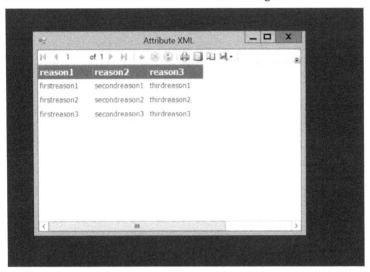

And here's the element XML version running in Visual Studio 2019:

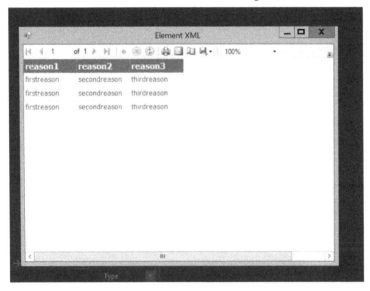

Question: Are there any providers that can be used to create reports that support XML?

Answer: Yes. There are two. MSDAOSP (The Microsoft Simple Data Provider) can be used like this:

```
Dim cn As New System.Data.OleDb.OleDbConnection
cn.ConnectionString = "Provider=MSDAOSP;Data Source = MSXML2.DSOCONTROL;"
cn.Open()
Dim cmd As New System.Data.OleDb.OleDbCommand()
cmd.Connection = cn
cmd.CommandType = System.Data.CommandType.Text
cmd.CommandText = "C:\Products.xml"
cmd.ExecuteNonQuery()
Dim Da As New System.Data.OleDb.OleDbDataAdapter(cmd)
Dim ds As New System.Data.DataSet
Da.Fill(ds)

For Each col As System.Data.DataColumn In ds.Tables(0).Columns

    Debug.Print(col.Caption)

Next
```

One issue with using this provider. It add an additional field: $text

```
ProductID
ProductName
SupplierID
CategoryID
QuantityPerUnit
UnitPrice
UnitsInStock
UnitsOnOrder
ReorderLevel
Discontinued
$Text
```

If you don't want to use the $Text in your reports, just don't add it when you create your report.

MSPersist uses a special kind of XML Generated when you use the ADODB.Recordset and save the recordset using the following code:

```
Dim rs As Object = CreateObject("ADODB.Recordset")
rs.ActiveConnection = "Provider=Microsoft.Jet.OLEDB.4.0;Data Source=C:\NWind.mdb"
rs.CursorLocation = 3
rs.LockType = 3
rs.Source = "Select * From Products"
rs.Open()
rs.Save("C:\ProductsSchema.xml", 1)
```

I would show you what the xml looks like but, it looks pretty scary. Suffice to say, the data is formatted as a row of attributes:

```
<z:row ProductID='1' ProductName='Chai' SupplierID='1' CategoryID='1' QuantityPerUnit='10 boxes x 20 bags'
UnitPrice='18' UnitsInStock='39' UnitsOnOrder='0' ReorderLevel='10' Discontinued='False'/>
```

Here's the code to use the generated XML with MSPersist:

```
Dim cn As New System.Data.OleDb.OleDbConnection
cn.ConnectionString = "Provider=MSPersist;"
cn.Open()
Dim cmd As New System.Data.OleDb.OleDbCommand()
cmd.Connection = cn
cmd.CommandType = System.Data.CommandType.Text
cmd.CommandText = "C:\ProductsSchema.xml"
cmd.ExecuteNonQuery()
Dim Da As New System.Data.OleDb.OleDbDataAdapter(cmd)
Dim ds As New System.Data.DataSet
Da.Fill(ds)

For Each col As System.Data.DataColumn In ds.Tables(0).Columns
    Debug.Print(col.Caption)
Next
```

Using the OleDbDataReader

Its fast but is it useable?

I've been putting this off for the end. Not because using the OleDbDataReader isn't worth using, but because the OleDbDataReader doesn't have any direct way to be used by the reports.

Furthermore, even if you wanted to work with it, For the information to be usable, you would have to convert it from the OleDbDataReader to a DataSet, DataTable or DataView.

Which, of course, begs, why even bother. I have no arguments to justify it either however, if you are pulling back a lot of data, then using it to build the structures or classes needed might just be a bit quicker than using the OleDbDataAdapter.

```
Dim cn As New System.Data.OleDb.OleDbConnection
cn.ConnectionString = "Provider=MSPersist;"
cn.Open()
Dim cmd As New System.Data.OleDb.OleDbCommand()
cmd.Connection = cn
cmd.CommandType = System.Data.CommandType.Text
cmd.CommandText = "C:\ProductsSchema.xml"
Dim dr As System.Data.OleDb.OleDbDataReader = cmd.ExecuteReader()

Dim dt As New System.Data.DataTable
For x = 0 To dr.FieldCount - 1
    dt.Columns.Add(dr.GetName(x))
Next
Do While (dr.Read)
    Dim drow As System.Data.DataRow = dt.NewRow()
    For x = 0 To dr.FieldCount - 1
        Dim v As String = dr.GetValue(x).ToString()
        drow(x) = v
    Next
    dt.Rows.Add(drow)
Loop
dt.AcceptChanges()

Debug.Print(dt.Columns.Count - 1)
Debug.Print(dt.Rows.Count - 1)
```

Using ADO with OleDb

Where the old meets the new

Believe it or not, the OleDbDataAdapter can take an ADODB.Recordset and convert it into a DataSet, DataTable or DataView. This is, again, another one of those why bother using it when you can just use OleDb?

Well, there's three reasons why I can think of off the top of my head.

First, you have legacy code that works perfectly fine and you want to add three lines of code to it and you're finished rewriting the code.

Second, you want to create and xsd file from your legacy code.

Third, you want to create some simple XML that you can use to create your reports.

Anyway, here's the code:

```
Dim rs As Object = CreateObject("ADODB.Recordset")
rs.ActiveConnection = "Provider=Microsoft.Jet.OLEDB.4.0;Data Source=C:\NWind.mdb"
rs.CursorLocation = 3
rs.LockType = 3
rs.Source = "Select * From Products"
rs.Open()
```

Using the DataSet:

```
Dim Da As New System.Data.OleDb.OleDbDataAdapter()
Dim ds As New System.Data.DataSet
Da.Fill(ds, rs, "Products")
```

Using the DataTable:

```
Dim Da As New System.Data.OleDb.OleDbDataAdapter()
Dim dt As New System.Data.DataTable
Da.Fill(dt, rs)

dt.TableName = "Products"
```

Using the DataView:

With the DataSet:

```
Dim dv As New System.Data.DataView = ds.Tables(0).DefaultView
```

With the DataTable:

```
Dim dv As New System.Data.DataView = dt.DefaultView
```

Some Last Thoughts and tips

About half way through this book I used what is known as an ISAM. ISAM is short for Indexed Sequential Access Method. Originally, the idea was to use a folder as the database and the files contained inside the folder were the tables.

But they can be both. Meaning some can have tables inside the file while others follow the original design. Furthermore, not all ISAMs are supported from the days of Microsoft.Jet.OleDb.3.51 to present: Microsoft.ACE.OleDb.16.0.

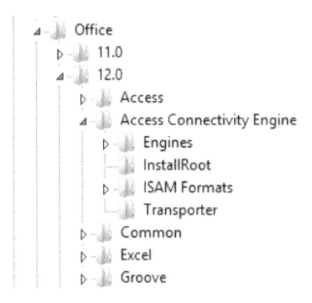

You will have to look in the registry: